GUITAR FOR BEGINNERS

LEARN TO PLAY YOUR FIRST SONG TODAY

BY: GUITAR NATION

Table of Contents

"Sometimes you'll want to give up the guitar. You'll hate the guitar. But if you stick with it, you're gonna be rewarded."

-Jimi Hendrix

Preface

The guitar, as seasoned and beginner musicians agree, is a unique instrument. An instrument renowned as a staple across genres. An instrument that undergoes a near-constant change in both style and capability. An instrument unhindered by the passage of time.

Though these statements are true, learning the guitar is not the difficult task it's made out to be. To that point, it's not a "task" at all. In fact, with this guide, it's easy. We know that learning the guitar revolves around a determined spirit combined with resources capable of answering your questions *before* you ask them.

And that's exactly what this guide aims to provide. A method that respects the human side of the guitar and amplifies your initial inspiration. Maybe you were enthralled by Slash's skilled hand in "Sweet Child O' Mine." Perhaps you found yourself pondering how YouTube pros create such powerful acoustic renditions of Top 40 songs. Whatever the case, you are more than capable of learning the guitar and this guide will give you everything you need to go from playing the air guitar to playing the actual guitar. Let's get started!

All About the Guitar

What kind of guitar is the best for a beginner?

So, you've decided that you want to master the fretboard. You've decided that against all else, you'll learn the not-so-difficult art of playing and creating music, the ultimate cross-cultural language. That said, what kind of guitar is best for a beginner?

Taking the first steps of your guitar journey and visiting your local music shop, you'll find a wide variety of six-string guitars ranging in price from $50 to $10,000+. They're beautiful, colorful, sleek, and come in many different variations. Though it's easy to be distracted by the frills and styles of these instruments, the first thing you need to know before buying is that guitars fall into two distinct categories: acoustic and electric guitars.

There are also subcategories of guitars that are important to discuss before hitting your local music shop. In the case of acoustic guitars, the two broad subcategories are steel-string acoustic guitars, and nylon-string (or classical guitars).

Both steel and nylon-string acoustics are excellent starter guitars as they require little additional equipment to play. The difference between these two guitar types, as you may have guessed, starts with a difference in the strings used with each guitar type.

Steel-string guitars are *always* used with steel or wound-steel strings. These strings are attached to the guitar in two locations: the bridge, and the tuning machines mounted on the headstock of the acoustic guitar. Steel-string acoustic guitars are often larger than electric guitars and feature a hollow-body formation, complete with a sound-hole placed between the body-end of the fingerboard and the top-mounted bridge. Steel-string guitars tend to feature thinner wooden necks than their classical guitar counterparts.

Nylon-string, or classical guitars *always* use nylon and nylon -wrapped wire strings. Nylon-string guitars tend to have a smaller body than steel-string guitars and feature a wider neck that typically doesn't feature any fingerboard markers.

Steel-string acoustic guitars tend to have a louder and brighter sound than classical guitars due to the types of strings they use. On the other hand, nylon-string guitars are frequently renowned for the quieter and warmer sound enjoyed in flamenco and classical guitar music.

These two general guitar categories, acoustic and electric, aim for the same result: music produced by picking, strumming, and fretting strings at the same time. Despite the similar outcome of produced sound, the acoustic and electric guitar deliver this result in different ways.

Without diving too deep into the realm of physics, acoustic guitars operate by absorbing and amplifying string vibrations (sound) within the guitar body. Strings are played, vibrations resonate through the body of the guitar, and the air within the guitar absorbs the vibrations. The resultant effect is the amplified or louder sound we know as music.

Electric guitars are an entirely different animal. They operate on similar principles of string vibrations, but looking at the electric guitar, you may notice a distinct lack of a sound hole. So, where do those chugging riffs and electrifying solos come from? The term "electric" guitar helps us clarify the answer.

Part one of that answer is, pickups. Pickups function like a sensitive microphone. They sit beneath the guitar strings and act as a transducer, converting string vibrations to an electrical signal. The cable connected to the guitar sends said signal to an amplifier, part two of our answer. The amplifier boosts the pickup signal and send it to the amp's output, where it reaches its final destination through the speakers within your amp. This process does become quite technical and includes a few more steps, especially when a chain of pedals is part of the set-up. But, for our purposes, just know that an electric guitar will need an amplifier to produce high-volume sound.

While pickups are commonly associated with electric guitars, it's important to note that some acoustic guitar models also feature pickups. This hybrid model is referred to as the acoustic-electric guitar. These guitars operate much like electric guitars, but have the added benefit of an acoustic sound at a higher, performance-friendly volume.

The Best Guitar for a Beginner

So, the question still stands, "What's better? Acoustic or electric?" And, like most matters of importance, the answer depends on a few aspects particular to learning and playing the guitar.

Acoustic guitars are often used as starter guitars because they're delivered ready to play. They don't require an amp which makes learning the guitar fast and convenient. Acoustic guitars are also perfect for mobile playing. Whether "mobile" means around your house, down the street, or around the world is up to you.

Despite the initial setup of an electric guitar and amplifier, electric guitars are also well-suited for novice guitarists. They often feature thinner strings that are easier to press down when compared to acoustic guitars. In addition, any electric guitar can be played into any electric guitar amplifier which lends itself to versatility down the road.

While both of these guitar types have their benefits, the best guitar type for a beginner isn't solely based on the category of the guitar you choose. The decision also includes budget considerations, musical preference, and personal style.

All of these aspects come into play when choosing a beginner guitar, but the most important consideration comes down to whether or not this guitar will keep you interested in learning.

There's a shared responsibility here, but your guitar, acoustic or electric, should always serve as a source of inspiration in your practice and performance. You'll never be disappointed if you choose a guitar that inspires you, suits your budget, and works with your favorite genres.

Parts of the Guitar

Neck

The neck, simply put, is the piece of the guitar that supports the fingerboard. The guitar neck is made from several wood species and features two sides; the flat side is for the fingerboard, and the rounded side is supporting the neck.

Headstock

The headstock, or the end of the guitar at the top of the neck, is primarily used to support tuning machines. Headstocks are far thinner than the acoustic and electric guitar bodies and come in a variety of shapes and sizes. In addition to supporting tuning machines, the headstock also acts as a brand identifier for most guitar manufacturers.

Tuning Machines

Guitar tuning machines are commonly made from a series of different metals and secure through the guitar's headstock in a series of six (or more, if the guitar has 7, 8, or 12 strings) evenly-spaced points. Each tuning machine includes a tuning knob, winding gears, and a metal cylinder. These components, paired with a small hole bored through each cylinder, are responsible for allowing the player to tune the instrument as well as securing strings to the guitar.

Nut

Where the fretboard meets the base of the headstock, guitars feature a thin piece of notched plastic, metal, wood, or sometimes bone. This component is referred to as the guitar's nut. Each notch along the nut houses one of the six strings. These notches provide even-string spacing along the fingerboard.

Fingerboard

The fingerboard is often what may come to mind when you think of a guitar's neck. Though they share the same position on the guitar, the purpose of the fingerboard is to provide a durable and playable surface responsible for changing the pitch of a played string. Between 21 and 25 individual spaces on the fingerboard are created by what are called "frets".

Frets

Frets are the individual metal strips beneath the strings of the guitar that segment the fingerboard. They are inserted across the width of a guitar's fingerboard, gradually increasing or decreasing the space between frets, depending on which direction you look at the guitar: as the pitch goes up, the space decreases; as the pitch goes down, the space increases. These separations represent individual note values, or frequencies, and consist of semitones, or half steps, in Western music.

*** It is important to recognize that while the frets separate the fingerboard into sections, they are also referred to when discussing note locations on the fingerboard. When saying a note is played on the "third fret", this means that the note is played on the space after the second and before the third fret, not on the third piece of metal from the headstock.

Guitar Body

Acoustic Guitars

The body of a guitar can vary widely depending on the guitar type in question.

Acoustic guitar bodies are made from joining larger pieces of formed and shaped wood braced with smaller supportive wood pieces. These combined pieces form a cavity within the guitar called the sound chamber. The sound chamber reverberates the resonating string vibrations and amplifies created sounds.

Electric Guitars

The form of an electric guitar's body is usually quite different than that of an acoustic guitar. Electric guitars come in one of three categories.

-Solid-body

-Semi-Hollow body

-Hollow body

Each of these guitar types features a unique sound that becomes a matter of preference as you progress in your study of the instrument. None of these guitar types are better than another, but rather, some qualities of each guitar suit some genres better than others. As an example, you wouldn't necessarily take a hollow-body jazz guitar to a metal gig, but again, the decision to play these guitars is preferential. No one is stopping you from taking a Guild to your Lamb of God cover band practice!

Solid-Body Guitars

The first category, solid-body electric guitars, is defined as an electric guitar body made from one or several pieces of solid material. This material is usually one or more species of wood such as maple or mahogany.

Solid-body guitars, like other electric guitars, feature pickups, volume and tone knobs to adjust the sound being directed toward the amp, and an input for your instrument cable. Some popular examples of the solid-body electric guitar include Fender's Telecaster®, Ibanez' RG-Series, and the Gibson or Epiphone Les Paul.

Semi-hollow bodies feature one or two hollow spots carved into the outer portions of the guitar body. These hollow spots are often exposed with "F-Holes" and accompany a centrally-supported wooden block running the vertical length of the guitar body called the tone block. The purpose of this configuration is to combine some of the resonant tone of acoustic guitars with the bright sound and amplification capability of solid-body electric guitars. This construction also works to reduce the amplifier feedback associated with hollow body guitars.

Some popular examples of the semi-hollow body include the Epiphone Dot and Gretsch's Electromatic® and Streamliner® Center-Block-series guitars.

Hollow-Body Guitars

Hollow-body guitars (formerly archtop electric guitars, designed before the introduction of magnetic pickups and amplifiers) feature a build similar to that of an acoustic guitar. Hollow-body electric guitars often feature several pickups in between the bridge and the guitar-side of the fingerboard. These pickups are typically bordered by several F-shaped sound holes called F-Holes, and work to combine acoustic guitar elements with an electric guitar sound.

Top

The guitar *belly*, or *top*, is essentially the "front" or "face" of acoustic and electric guitar bodies. Electric guitar tops are recognized by top-mounted pickups, while acoustic tops are recognized by carved sound holes beneath the strings.

While the guitar top of both acoustic and electric guitars serves to provide beautifully simple or ornate designs, the acoustic top's main job is absorbing string vibration and transferring this vibration into the sound chamber.

The top of an acoustic is commonly made of a strong, yet pliable wood, like spruce. The species of wood used to make guitar tops are chosen carefully. They must be able to absorb vibrations and effectively vibrate the air within the sound chamber as well as the outside air to produce music.

Sound Hole

The sound hole, most commonly associated with acoustic guitars, is what allows amplified sound to escape from the sound chamber when playing guitar. The sound hole is often circular and typically measures around 3-4" in diameter.

Back

The back of the acoustic guitar serves two purposes. One, it completes the enclosure of the sound chamber along with the guitar top and guitar sides. Secondly, the back also acts much like the guitar top as a soundboard. These two shaped pieces of wood absorb string vibration and work to amplify the vibrations created by the player.

In the case of semi-hollow and hollow-body guitars, the back provides supporting structure for the internal parts and pieces such as the tone block and wooden bracings. Solid-body electric guitars have an area within the body carved out for their electronic components.

Sides

In acoustic and some electric guitar models, the sides work together with the guitar top and back to form a sound chamber where string vibration is amplified, creating the sound of the guitar as we know it today. Manufacturers tend to have specific methods of producing their acoustic, semi-hollow, and hollow-body guitars, but the sides are always affixed to the top and back of the guitar regardless of the manufacturer's preferred construction.

Bridge

When searching for your ideal six-string, you may notice that the strings on any guitar model are connected to the guitar by the tuning machines and continue down the guitar to a wooden or metal support. This wooden or metal support is called the *bridge*.

Bridges on acoustic guitars and electric guitars look and function differently.

Electric Guitar Bridges

Electric guitar bridges are typically made from steel or aluminum components that are fastened to the guitar top or routed portions of the guitar body. These components maintain string height across the body and fingerboard, allowing for smaller, incremental adjustments to the guitar's tuning, and work with the tuning machines to keep the strings attached to the guitar.

Any electric guitar at your local guitar shop will come with either a vibrato or fixed bridge set-up. In a general sense, the two bridge types are similar as they both support the guitar strings, but the bridge styles have some important differences.

Vibrato-Bridge Electric Guitars

Often called a "tremolo" or "whammy bar" bridge, a vibrato bridge allows a guitarist to add vibrato to individual strings or entire chords by pressing down or pulling up on the vibrato bar. Legendary guitarists such as Eddie Van Halen, Jimi Hendrix, Brian May of Queen, and more recently John Petrucci of Dream Theater, all implement the vibrato bar to embellish their guitar playing.

Through-Body Vibrato Bridges

To start, guitars built with a through-body vibrato bridge—such as models produced by Fender and Ibanez—will have a fitted hole routed from the top to the back of the guitar to house the vibrato bridge components. These components include a back-mounted spring plate, bridge posts, the bridge itself, and several springs to connect the bridge to the spring plate.

The vibrato bridge is inserted into the routed portion of the guitar body where it's mounted on the bridge posts. The bridge is then connected to the spring plate on the back of the guitar with the metal springs.

Springs? Yes, you read that correctly. Springs.

Because vibrato bridges raise and lower the pitch of the guitar strings by angling the bridge toward or away from the neck, the string tension produced by tightening strings with the tuning machines must be counterbalanced by some force. A series of three to five springs connected to the bridge and the spring plate provides this force.

Once all components are connected, the mounting posts act as a fulcrum point, allowing the guitarist to raise and lower the pitch of the guitar strings by either pulling up or depressing the vibrato bar. Each vibrato bridge sits parallel to the guitar body in neutral position, until angled toward or away from the guitar neck. This bridge angle is produced with a vibrato, tremolo, or whammy bar or arm, of which the terms are often used interchangeably, that screws or snaps into each vibrato bridge.

Unlike the use of the manual vibrato technique (raising and lowering a string's pitch repeatedly), the vibrato bar allows a guitarist to add vibrato to all the guitar strings simultaneously.

The Stratocaster® or "Strat" is an extremely common example of a guitar with a vibrato bridge that many novice guitarists cut their teeth on.

Stratocaster® Vibrato Bridge - Front

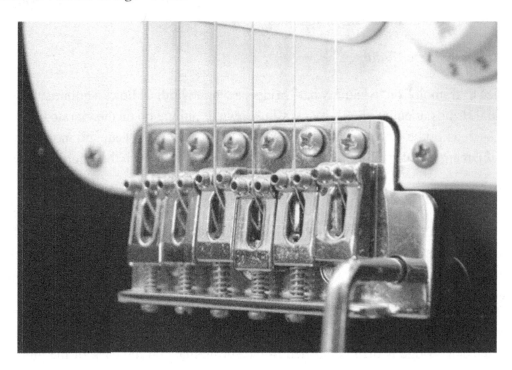

The two photos of the Stratocaster® above show the strings passing through the bridge and heading toward the tuning machines on the headstock. In the image below, we can see the string holes where the strings are inserted and where they connect to the back side of the guitar.

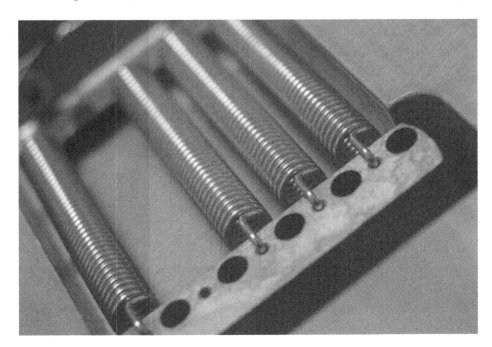

Top-Loaded Vibrato Bridges

While the through-body vibrato bridge is a common sight in the guitar community, top-loaded vibrato bridges produced by manufacturers like Gretsch, Epiphone, and Guild also enjoy continued use by many guitarists today.

Top-loaded vibrato bridges are installed on the top of the guitar and consist of two main components: The bridge and saddle system seen directly behind the pickup in the above photo, and the spring-loaded vibrato system placed behind the bridge and saddle.

In this bridge configuration, the strings first connect to a metal roller bar placed within the bridge. The strings wrap around this roller bar where they rest on the bridge and saddles and continue on down to the tuning machines. The spring-loaded vibrato arm rotates the roller bar toward the neck to reduce string tension and away from the neck to increase string tension.

Fixed-Bridge Electric Guitars

The fixed bridge remains in a static position once it's installed on the guitar body. Unlike vibrato-style bridges, a guitarist can't actively alter the pitch of the guitar strings through the fixed bridge.

Although the fixed-bridge design is fairly intuitive, there are a few design preferences guitar designers and manufacturers use within the bridge category. The first of which is the *through-body* fixed bridge.

Through-Body Fixed Bridges

The name "through-body" bridge refers to how the strings are fed *through* the evenly-spaced string holes that have been drilled through the guitar body. Once inserted in the back of the guitar, the guitar strings will be pushed through the holes where they will come out of the bridge plate, or from behind the bridge. These strings are then supported by *saddles*, or the metal pieces that help keep the strings at comfortable string height.

In the image of this Telecaster® below, we can see how the strings come up through the bridge plate and rest on the saddles before they're connected to the tuning machines.

Telecaster®

The Top-Loaded Fixed Bridge

Another subset of bridges in the fixed-bridge category is the top-loaded bridge. The term "top-loaded" means that the guitar strings are secured to either the top-mounted bridge components or a tailpiece placed behind the bridge and toward the bottom of the guitar. Guitar strings don't pass through the guitar body in a top-loaded bridge.

The *Tune-O-Matic™* bridge is one of the most common bridges within the top-loaded bridge category. Originally developed by Gibson Brands, Inc. in the mid-20th century, the Tune-O-Matic™ bridge design is still used on current guitar models like the Les Paul®, SG®, and ES®-series hollow-body guitars.

Tune-O-Matic™ Bridge

Tune-O-Matic™ Bridge - Les Paul®

In the picture above, the Tune-O-Matic™ bridge is mounted between the bridge pickup (furthest from the neck) and a metal tailpiece called the stop bar or stop tail. The stop bar is positioned on the left side of the photo above with the bridge following immediately to the right of the stop bar. Both the bridge and the stop bar are secured onto the guitar top by adjustable metal posts.

In the Tune-O-Matic™ set-up, the strings are connected to the guitar by first feeding them through equally-spaced string holes bored through the tailpiece. The strings are then drawn over the Tune-O-Matic bridge and ultimately connect at the tuning machines on the headstock.

Overall, the fixed bridge, whether through-body or top-loaded, is a low-maintenance and easily re-strung bridge, making it a popular choice for beginners.

Acoustic Guitar Bridges

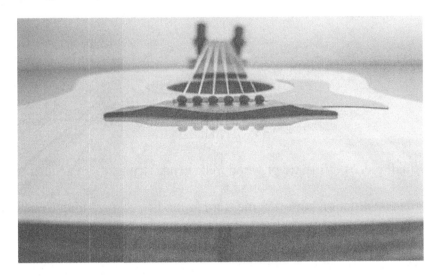

Acoustic guitar bridges are used to keep the strings on the guitar, provide even string height across the guitar body and neck, and transfer string vibrations into the top of the guitar. These bridges are installed on the top of the guitar behind the sound hole. Acoustic bridges are typically made from a shaped wooden base paired with a plastic or bone saddle. Holes are drilled within the wooden base to allow strings to be secured to the guitar with bridge pins.

Bridge Pins

Bridge pins are small pieces of plastic or wood that secure strings to an acoustic guitar.

Bridge pins vary in construction but often measure around 1" to 1½"-long by 1/8" wide to secure strings. The ball-end of the string is inserted into the string hole and the bridge pin is inserted afterward to hold the string in place. Once secured to the tuning machine, the string is wound around the pin and proper tension is achieved.

Strap Buttons

Both acoustic and electric guitars include strap buttons to allow the player to play in both seated or standing positions. Strap buttons are made of metal, plastic, or wood, and install on the sides on the back of the guitar.

Strings

Strings serve a fundamental, but simple function on the guitar. Despite their simplicity, there are numerous traits to choose from: thickness, material, and other components based on the guitar type. To better explain the many variations of guitar strings that blanket music stores carry, let's take a closer look at how strings are made and which guitars they're used for.

String Materials

Electric Guitar Strings

Electric guitar strings are commonly made from steel, nickel, and alloys of the two. Each string varies in construction, with the thicker strings, such as the sixth, fifth, and fourth, featuring a thin piece of wire wound around a solid core. These strings typically employ lighter and easier-to-press string thicknesses than acoustics and provide exceptional signal conduction for pickups.

Acoustic Guitar Strings

Acoustic guitar strings are often constructed with bronze or brass-wrapped steel wires. This wrapping technique, and the metals used in these strings, allows for better volume so the acoustic can "cut through the mix."

String Type

In your search for the perfect guitar, you may have noticed that both acoustic and electric guitars often use metal strings. It would make sense to assume that, because they both use metal strings, the strings could be used interchangeably. While this is logical, an underlying problem remains.

Using the same strings for electric and acoustic guitars can be broken down into two sub-issues. First, different strings have different magnetic properties. Second, string gauges for each guitar type tend to differ widely.

As we already know, electric guitars use pickups. These pickups operate on principles of magnetism and some guitar strings are more magnetic than others. Acoustic guitar strings are often made from metals like bronze and brass that don't conduct a proper signal and will result in a quieter sound from an amplifier.

Acoustic string gauge, or thickness, also tends to be thicker than most electric guitar string gauges. This is because thicker strings tend to produce string vibrations at louder volumes when compared to thinner strings.

Although it may seem logical to have thicker, louder strings on an electric guitar, we have to remember that thicker strings are harder to play. They might be louder due to the string thickness, but we can't play loudly if we can't press the strings down. Also, electric guitar pickups and amplifiers are (please don't tell your neighbors we told you this) doing the heavy lifting in terms of volume. Volume is ultimately increased by the guitar and the amp, not by string thickness.

All in all, it's a good idea to keep the two string types separate: use acoustic strings for acoustic guitars and electric strings for electric guitars.

String Gauge

Getting the right set of strings for your guitar comes with some knowledge of how string manufacturers describe their products. Some common string gauge measurement includes the terms *extra light, light medium, heavy,* and *extra heavy*.

While it would make sense that these terms provide a general definition of the strings they're describing, the truth is, they don't. String gauge is measured in terms of thousandths of an inch, which serves as a much more reliable baseline to understand string thickness. If we consider a common "High-E" string gauge, what we're really looking at as a thickness measurement of 1011 thousandths of an inch (0.0010-0.0011). These gauges are commonly referred to as a 10's and 11's, respectively.

While this system can be frustrating, it's a good idea to take a look at the thickness of the high-E string in any pack of strings and purchase accordingly.

As a rule of thumb, remember that thinner string gauges require less pressure to press down and are easier to play when compared to thicker string gauges.

Guitar Accessories

Guitar Picks

Guitar picks are small pieces of material, often plastic, that guitarists use to pluck the strings on the guitar. Pick thickness is measured in millimeters (mm) and is selected based on the player's preference and style of play. Generally, these thicknesses are put into broad sizes, which include:

Thin: .44mm
Medium: .45-.69mm
Heavy: .85-1.20mm
Thick: 1.5mm+

Guitar picks feature a shape that often resembles that of a rounded triangle, though other shapes like pointed ovals are available.

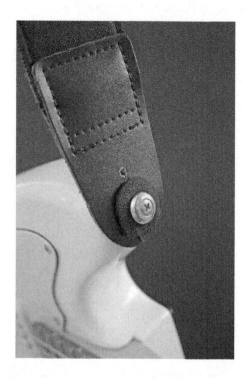

Guitar straps are used when playing the guitar in a standing position, though some guitarists use them while sitting down to play (in fact, it is recommended to wear a strap when playing in any position for proper ergonomics). Straps are often made from leather, nylon, or other fabric materials and attach to the guitar on two strap buttons on opposing sides of the guitar body. To secure a strap, the guitarist attaches one end of the strap to one strap button near the bottom of the acoustic or electric guitar. The guitarist then drapes the guitar strap over his or her shoulder and attaches the opposite end of the strap to the second strap button.

Instrument cable

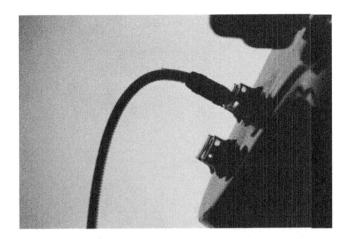

Instrument cables provide the connection between pickup-equipped guitars and amplifiers, resulting in increased signal volume. The standard cable used with electric and acoustic-electric guitars features a 1/4" phone connector on both ends of the cable. Both ends of the cable are suitable for either the guitar or the amplifier.

Cleaning cloth

As you play the guitar, you may find that sweat and dust start to accumulate on the body, fingerboard, and other areas beneath the strings. A cleaning cloth is a quick solution to remedy the muck that builds up overtime. When choosing a cleaning cloth, it's important to choose a material that is safe for the finish of your guitar such as microfiber, pure and untreated flannel, or suede.

Tuner

A guitar tuner is absolutely essential as you begin your guitar journey. Guitar tuners allow you to tune to a precise pitch and typically come in three different categories. These include microphone-based digital tuners, vibration-based clip-on tuners, and line-in tuners.

In the later sections of this guide we'll go over the whole process of <u>How to Tune Your Guitar</u> to make sure your guitar is tuned accurately every time you pick it up.

But, for now, here's the short version:

Each of the guitar strings has a corresponding pitch or note it's normally tuned to. Guitar tuners measure the pitch of the guitar strings and immediately tell us whether or not the strings are tuned to the note they're supposed to be tuned to. Tuning with a guitar tuner makes sure our guitar is prepared for practice, making learning far easier, faster, and more fun. As beginner guitarists, you couldn't ask for a more useful tool.

It's important to note that some guitar tuners work better with acoustic guitars than electrics and vice versa. If you have an acoustic guitar, we recommend using a microphone or vibration-based tuner because acoustic guitars don't have the ability to send a signal through an instrument cable. For those with electric guitars, any of these tuners will work but we recommend a line-in or vibration-based tuner as they tend to provide a truer tune despite the low-volume output of the electric guitars.

Extra Strings

As you begin to experiment with the guitar, you may notice that your strings start to sound dull and even corrode over time. This is completely normal but will decrease the quality of your sound and may make the strings uncomfortable to play. It is a good idea to keep a couple packs of your preferred brand of strings around in the event that you need to replace them for corrosion reasons or when strings break.

Guitar Travel Cases

If you plan to take your guitar from one location to the next, investing in a gig-bag or a hard-shell case is a smart decision. That said, understanding the difference and the benefits the two types of travel cases provide is key to protecting your instrument in a budget-friendly manner.

Gig-bag

Gig-bags are often made from padded nylon and enclose the instrument with a metal zipper. They are ideal for quick transport over short distances as they are lightweight and quite thin. In addition to a slight, efficient build, gig-bags are an economical option for a guitar case. If you elect to purchase a gig-bag we recommend only transporting the guitar when you have direct supervision over the instrument itself.

Hard-shell Case

Hard-shell cases are a preferred option for musicians who want to transport their instrument to lessons, practices, or performances without worry of instrument damage. Hard-shell cases feature a hardened exterior, interior padding to reduce shock impact to the instrument, and a plush lining to maintain the surface of the instrument. Most hard-shell cases feature multiple securing points on the outside of the guitar and frequently include a locking mechanism for further security.

Before You Begin: The Basics

How to Hold the Guitar

You've got your guitar, your accessories like picks and tuners, and you're ready to play. While jumping in and strumming like a fiend seems like the right choice, it's important to think about how we hold the guitar and how our bad posture can inhibit our playing.

You may be thinking "Posture? I just want to play!"

And that is a great attitude to take to the guitar. That said, improper posture can lead to a slew of unnecessary problems like back and neck pain, repetitive motion injuries (RMIs), carpal tunnel syndrome, and the dreaded *MUTED STRINGS*.

This section will detail the right and not-so-difficult steps to make sure you can play comfortably, practice efficiently, and learn more, provided your fingertips will allow it!

<u>Proper Posture While Sitting Down</u>

To achieve proper posture while sitting and playing, you need a few things: an obstruction-free practice space; a comfortable chair, preferably without armrests, that allows us to play the guitar with your knees bent at around 90-degrees; your back straight, and your arms unrestrained; and of course, your guitar.

Once you have these elements, go ahead, and take a seat with your six-string.

Your feet should be about shoulder-width apart with your knees positioned around a 90-degree bend. Our backs should be straight but relaxed.

Your guitar, acoustic or electric, should be placed on the same leg as your strumming or picking hand. Each guitar model has a slight inward, concave curve on either side of the body that will sit comfortably on this leg (this curve also attributes to the inner-acoustics of an acoustic guitar; the curved shape helps break up the bouncing sound reflections). You'll want the guitar's pickups or sound hole facing away from you as you rest the guitar on your leg. It's important to note that the guitar's weight should *not* be supported by your fretting hand; ideally, you want the guitar's weight to be balanced on your leg to allow our hands to play the instrument freely, rather than lift it up and down.

For classical, fingerstyle guitar playing, the guitar is typically seated on the leg closer to the strings. This helps keep the hand and fingers in an ideal position and reduce the risk of injury. However, this position is not recommended for typical guitar playing, since it involves consistent strumming motions from the arm and wrist.

29

With your guitar in place and your body comfortable, it's time to talk about how your arms interact with the guitar to keep proper posture. Your strumming arm should drape over the top-rear section of the guitar. If you get this positioning right, your strumming hand should fall naturally above the strings.

Your fretting arm, the arm opposite of the strumming arm should sit around a 90-degree bend at the elbow, similar to your knees. This angle allows us to comfortably reach the guitar neck while keeping a straight wrist.

As you start to learn the chords, melodies, and scales in this book, you may notice your posture start to change. That's okay! Some of the techniques may be hard to implement without full visibility of the fingerboard. That said, remember that a large part of learning the guitar and making learning easier, comes from proper posture.

Pro tip: Position a mirror so you can see your "fretting" hand; make sure that your wrist stays straight!

Proper Hand Position

Both your right and left hands are used when playing the guitar. One hand, the *fretting hand*, is responsible for fretting or pressing down the strings. The other hand, the *picking* or *strumming hand,* is responsible for strumming or picking the strings on the opposite end of the guitar.

Fretting Hand

While keeping the posture we've described above, you want your fretting hand to hold the guitar neck so it falls in between where your fingers connect to the palm of your hand.

As you play, you may notice the neck lift away from our palm. This is normal. Just be sure to keep your wrist straight as you fret notes and chords and you'll be golden.

Strumming Hand

Your strumming hand should rest just above the center of the guitar *top* and slightly behind the sound hole in acoustics, or the center-point of your pickups in electric guitars.

Proper Finger Position

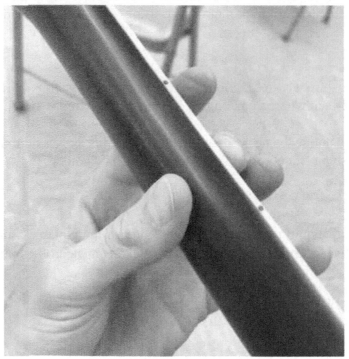

To get the most out of your guitar playing, you want the fingers of your fretting hand to be properly positioned. You want to keep your fretting hand in the same position described previously and start to add your fingers in two sections – thumb and your other four fingers.

Your thumb should be placed centrally on the back side of the neck with your fretting arm resting around 90-degrees. Please note that some techniques may change this positioning. This is okay, but returning to this position is a must to maintain proper finger position.

Once your thumb is in place, you want to curl your other four fingers onto the fingerboard. Your fingertips should now be pointed toward the strings and fingerboard.

Imagine that you're making the letter "C" with your fretting hand to get your fingers to curve comfortably, and to get your thumb in a relaxed and supportive position.

Proper Posture While Standing Up

Although it may feel very different, the proper posture you use when standing and playing is quite similar to how you play when we sit down and play the guitar. You need to keep your back straight, our shoulders square, and our feet about shoulder width apart.

Your guitar, suspended on your shoulder by a guitar strap, should rest around your mid-section. A good baseline for proper posture is making sure the sound hole or the center point between pickups lines up with your belly-button. Though some more advanced guitarists tend to raise or lower their guitars and straps for the stylistic appeal, it's a good idea to keep your guitar centered as it is easier to play when centered on your mid-section.

As always, make sure your wrist on your fretting hand remains straight when holding the guitar neck.

<u>Proper Hand Position</u>

The way we use our hands when we play standing up is similar to how we play sitting down. Your fretting hands need to grasp the neck of the guitar, ensuring the neck falls where your fingers connect to your palm. However, the two positions differ is in the strumming hand.

When standing up, you may find that your strumming arm rests lower than it does in the seated position. To ensure proper posture, keep your strumming arm relaxed and allow it to rest atop the closest side of the guitar. Like your seated posture, your strumming hand should rest just above the guitar strings, around the center point between the bridge and the sound hole or pickups.

<u>Proper Finger Position</u>

For the most part, the thumb should remain centered on the back of the neck. However, certain chords and positions on the fretboard will put your thumb in an awkward position. Just remember to prioritize a straight wrist over a centered thumb for these occasions. Your four "fretting" fingers should be curled and relaxed.

How to Hold a Pick

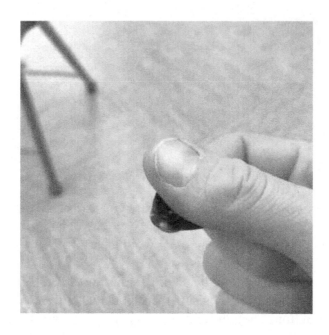

At first, holding a flat guitar pick seems unnatural, but proper picking is quite easy when we look at how we hold the pick.

The flat guitar pick, or flat-pick, is traditionally held between and played with your thumb and index and/or middle finger. The easiest way to identify the proper pick positioning is to take your thumb and index finger and press them (lightly) together so they meet in a cross pattern. Your index finger should be pointed downward, and the soft part of your thumb should cross the pad of your index finger horizontally.

Once you've achieved this position, grab a pick and place it between these two fingers. The pointed end of the pick should follow the direction of your index finger, though some angles are more comfortable for some guitarists than others.

It is also important to note that the picking and strumming motions employed by guitarists do not come explicitly from the fingers. Rather, they stem from combined motions involving up-and-down strumming from the elbow, motions from the wrist, as well as some motion directed by the picking fingers themselves.

Proper Picking Depth

A common frustration of many novice guitarists is a lack of fluidity in their picking hand. To correct this problem, we need to look at our picking hand and, particularly how deeply we're inserting the guitar pick in between the guitar strings.

When you play, you should place the guitar pick deep enough to pluck the string, and shallow enough to maximize maneuverability between different strings. For most guitarists, this will fall naturally between one-sixteenth and one-eighth of an inch; of course, the exact picking depth used will vary from guitarist to guitarist. Stevie Ray Vaughan had huge hands while Angus Young of AC/DC had meager mitts. Regardless, they've both managed to wrangle their picking hands by focusing on depth to the point where it takes no consideration at all.

Achieving this state of muscle memory takes time and should not be your main focal point when playing the guitar. As you study this guide, be sure to focus on playing the chords, melody, and music first, checking up on your picking hand as difficulties arise.

How to Tune Your Guitar

So far, we've covered all of the parts of the guitar, the useful guitar accessories, and the right posture to use when playing the guitar, but this is all for naught if we can't tune the instrument. This section will cover the basics of guitar tuning, the most common guitar tuning, and how to tune your guitar to itself if you don't have a tuner.

What is Tuning?

Tuning, as it relates to guitar and other stringed instruments, means to increase or decrease string tension to achieve a desired pitch for each string. These pitches are often described in a general term like *standard tuning* to tell us, in shorthand, what pitch each guitar string will be tuned to.

Why is Tuning Important?

There are a few reasons why tuning is important. Firstly, an out of tune guitar sounds just plain bad. The notes of each string don't match up very well and playing the guitar, no matter how great of a guitarist they are, won't sound all that great. Second, tuning the guitar to a set of generally agreed upon notes, like *standard tuning* in the next section, allows us to recreate songs that others have written, in the tuning they were originally written.

Standard Tuning and When You Should Tune

When we say a guitar is tuned to standard tuning, it means that each string is tuned to a series of notes used in the many different genres of music. This tuning has been accepted and used by guitarists for decades.

This is often easier to visualize when referring to a guitar. Look at this picture for example.

On a six-string guitar, and any guitar for that matter, we use a series of letters and numbers as reference points to discuss each string and their respective tuning.

The strings in this image are numbered from left-to-right, or thickest to thinnest, as, "6th, 5th, 4th, 3rd, 2nd, 1st". The lettering system follows this numbering from left-to-right. "E, A, D, G, B, E"

When you start playing guitar, this system can take some time to commit to memory. To make it easier, using an acronym can make remembering standard tuning far easier. One we prefer is as follows:

6th (E)ddie- 5th (A)te- 4th (D)ynamite- 3rd (G)ood- 2nd (B)ye- 1st (E)ddie.

Tuning, though it can be done by comparing your guitar to the pitch of other instruments or even YouTube videos, is far easier (and more accurate) when done with a tuner. Using any tuner, whether microphone, line-in, or otherwise, allows you to visualize the current tuning of your instrument and perform small adjustments until you achieve your desired string pitches.

Tuning the instrument does take time, but it should be the first thing you do whenever you pick up the guitar. Tuning the guitar before we play ensures that everything we practice has a reliable basis of even string pitches. This means that, because everything else is evenly tuned, it becomes easier to identify odd sounds during our practice sessions than if our guitar were out of tune.

Your "musical ear" needs to learn what notes and chords sound like when they are in tune. If you play an instrument that's out of tune, you aren't giving your musical ear a chance to learn.

Tuning Basics

In this section, we'll be tossing a few musical terms around that may or may not be familiar to you. These include *pitch*, *sharp*, and *flat*, which are central terms in regards to tuning the guitar.

When we talk about *pitch*, we're talking about specific measurements of vibration speed, or frequency, that tell us how slow or fast something vibrates and how low or high the frequency of said vibration is. These specific pitch measurements or frequencies are referred to as "notes" in music. In short, pitch operates in-sync with frequency: The higher the frequency, the higher the pitch, the lower the frequency, the lower the pitch.

As we tune each of our guitar strings, we're effectively increasing or decreasing the string's vibration speed, by increasing and decreasing tension with the tuning machines. If, for example, the frequency of a note is higher, the pitch of the note will be higher as well. The same can be said for lower notes, frequencies (vibrations), and pitches.

As we increase or decrease string's pitch and tension when tuning, we're doing so to ensure each of our strings needs is set to the desired pitch. This is solely based on the tuning, or set of notes, you have decided for your guitar. In cases where our string is below our desired pitch, the string's pitch is considered *flat*. In cases where our string is above the desired pitch, the string's pitch is considered *sharp*.

All in all, the main goal with tuning each time you pick up the guitar is a simple one. It's making sure your strings match the pitches given by desired tuning and allow your instrument to sound good both on its own and when playing with other people.

Using a Line-In, Microphone-Based, or Clip-On Tuner

Please note that these tuning methods will be detailed for use with a right-handed guitar. If you're using a left-handed guitar, please complete these steps with the opposite tuning knob rotations.

To properly tune your guitar to standard tuning with line-in, mic-based, and clip-on tuners, you first need to turn the tuner on and bring the guitar close to microphone tuner, plug your electric guitar into the line-in tuner, or attach clip-on tuner to the headstock of your guitar. Music cables used with line-in tuners should be plugged into the guitar and the tuner to transfer the guitar's signal to the tuner (make sure you unplug it when you're finished playing so the batteries don't die!).

Once you're set up, try playing the thickest (6th), or E-string. Did the string's note register on the tuner? If the digital display lights up and it returns a letter, you're headed in the right direction!

Now we want to take that letter displayed on the tuner and compare it to the main character in our unfortunate standard tuning initialism – **Eddie** Ate Dynamite, Good-Bye Eddie – and tune that 6th string to the letter E. Follow the E-string to where it connects at the tuning machine head on your guitar's headstock. If this is your first time tuning your guitar, you'll more than likely be either flat (string pitch is too low), or sharp (string pitch is too high).

Once you've identified your low E-string's current pitch, you can adjust the string tension until it's at a proper E-note. If your string is currently flat, you want to look at your tuning machines on the headstock of the guitar.

On your guitar's headstock, you should see some tuning knobs that fall right in line with the position of each tuning machine. Locate the tuning knob associated with the low E-string. Now you need to start adjusting your pitch by increasing or decreasing tension on the low E-string. If your string's pitch is lower than the desired E-note, or flat, you need to start increasing string tension by rotating the low E-string tuning knob *counterclockwise*. If your string's pitch is higher than the desired E-note, or sharp, we need to decrease string tension by rotating the same tuning knob *clockwise*.

While the low E-string is fairly thick when compared to the other five strings, it's important to take this process slowly. Whether your string's pitch is sharp or flat, be sure to keep an eye on the tuner to get as close as possible to the desired pitch.

After you've tuned the E-string to the proper pitch "E", continue this process with 5th and 4th strings. Once you have these strings tuned to E, A, and D, we need to discuss tuning the last three strings.

Depending on what type of guitar you have, and more importantly, how your headstock is configured, these next steps may vary on how to proceed. If your guitar has **all six** tuning machines on **one side** of the headstock, you can go ahead and continue tuning as we have been, with clockwise rotations for sharp-string pitch and counterclockwise for flat-string pitch for the remaining strings.

If your guitar has three tuning machines on either side of the headstock, you need to reverse your adjustment rotation for the tuning knobs on the new side. For guitars with the G, B, and E (or 3rd, 2nd, and 1st-string) tuning knobs on the opposite side of the E, A, and D string tuning machines, the adjustment rotation will be clockwise for flat strings and counterclockwise for sharp strings.

No Tuner? No Problem

There may be times where you've misplaced your tuner or times where you don't have a tuner at all. In either case, there is a method that can easily take care of your tuning needs.

***A Note on this Tuning Method:* Because it relies on a potentially "untuned" reference note (the low-E or sixth string), this method should be used as a last resort, especially when you're learning to play the guitar. That isn't to say that this method won't "work," but using this method "tunes" the guitar to a potentially untuned string. You may notice the inconsistency of this method when playing along to songs or exercises on your computer, smartphone, or other audio devices.

The method we'll be using will rely on your ear to compare two pitches on separate strings and decide whether or not the two pitches sound similar. To start this method, we'll begin with the thickest E-string on your guitar. Go ahead and play it to test its tuning. If this string is loose, buzzy, or wiggles around when you play it, go ahead and tighten that baby right up. Once you've increased the string's tension with the tuning knob, take a look at the 5th fret on our guitar. On most guitars, this will be marked with the first fingerboard marker or inlay closest to your guitar's headstock.

Fret the low-E string on the 5th fret and pluck the string. Next, play the open-5th string. Now, play both of these notes and allow them to ring out together. Are they similar in pitch? Odds are, if the guitar is relatively tuned, the sounds will be similar in pitch. This is because the 5th fret on the E-string is actually an A-note, the same note as the open-5th string. We want to take these two sounds and adjust the A-string tuning knob until the pitches are the same between the two open and fretted strings. This may require reaching over with your picking hand to adjust the tuning peg.

Next, we'll complete the same steps as before for the remaining strings; fret the A string on the 5th fret and compare the resulting pitch to the open-D string. Make sure to let both strings ring out at the same time and compare the two notes. Like before, we want to tune these two strings to be as close as possible to each other.

Repeat these steps to tune the G string; play and hold out the 5th fret of the D string, and play the open G string at the same time and tune them so they match.

Once the G string is tuned, we need to tune the B string. Though it would make sense to follow the previous steps and tune the whole guitar that way, we need to make one minor adjustment to our process.

To tune the B string, instead of fretting the 5th fret of our G string, we'll fret the 4th fret. From there, the process for matching the pitches between these two strings is exactly the same.

Finally, to tune the E string, return to the original 5th fret position on the B string and follow the instructions for the A, D, and G strings above.

Developing the Right Mindset

Practice, Routine, Discipline, Goals, Little Victories, Mastery?

As with learning any new skill, learning to play the guitar becomes far easier when we first incorporate the right mindset. The player's mindset really comes down to one quality that outweighs all else: *discipline*. Unlike motivation, discipline is the force that acts against all procrastination. Discipline is a series of ingrained habits, banishing the "I'll do it tomorrows" and Netflix binges.

But taking the study of the guitar as a discipline isn't exactly easy, per se. To do it effectively, we need to look at a few key ingredients: practice consistency, practice environment, and a healthy reward system.

1.) Play at the same time, for the same amount of time, every day.

Setting a specific time aside for guitar each day allows you to choose when you'll feel most comfortable and alert when playing. It could be when you wake up in the morning. It could be when your neighbors would be less than delighted to hear your serenades. Regardless of the specific time, adhering to a convenient play time for your schedule will bring lasting success in your guitar studies; be consistent and hold yourself accountable for your practice time.

2.) Make sure you're practicing the guitar in a comfortable space.

In many cases, creative work and the practice of such, is personal. It's reflective of what you're willing to put into the instrument, which can feel vulnerable. Therefore, having a practice space that doesn't impede your learning and creativity is paramount when you begin playing. Find somewhere that is free of distraction, contains only the minimal, essential items needed for practice, and consider creating some kind of "vibe" for this sacred space. A candle can add this atmosphere, and eventually its smell will be associated in your mind with playing guitar.

3.) Celebrate the little victories!

The guitar, with all of its positives, can be a pain at times. It can be endlessly frustrating because your mind is able to comprehend concepts quickly, but your body needs more time! There may be times when you just need one finger to get in the right spot and it just... won't! But being patient is what will get you through. It also helps to set goals, piecemeal and celebrate the completion of those goals; this can make learning fun rather than something to expect. You can reward yourself intrinsically by taking some time to reflect on how much you've learned, extrinsically by gifting yourself a new guitar "toy" when completing a certain number of exercises, or learning a new song. Of course, any version of these types of ideas will work best if *you make it for yourself.*

In the next section, we'll go over some chords and, while we have some ideas about how they should be learned, we'll prompt you to consider what way makes YOU feel good about learning them. Isn't that the point of playing the guitar anyway?

Overall, each guitarist is different. Although Tony Iommi of Black Sabbath and Keith Urban play the guitar, they play the guitar *very* differently. The same goes for anyone starting out on the guitar. Each guitarist takes a similar but different approach to learning, and becoming intimidated by the development or skill level of your friends or heroes ultimately defeats the purpose of learning the guitar and making music. Don't be disappointed by your progress. Learning the guitar takes time. If it takes you five minutes to master the "D" chord, congratulations. If it takes you a month, that's fine too. Be patient with yourself; if you're always on the lookout for the positives in guitar, then the guitar will never, ever, fail you.

Finally, don't fear failure.

We all failed at the start. As much as I hate to say it, Jimi Hendrix probably wasn't soothing ears when he began playing the guitar. The point is, over time, these tools and tips will build upon one another and result in enjoyment and knowledge of the guitar.

First Things First: How to Read Guitar Tablature

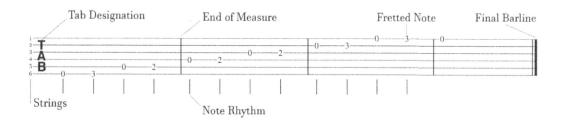

Tablature is an effective source for learning many different songs across many different genres. It uses a simple grid pattern consisting of several horizontal lines to indicate strings. This string notation is separated by vertical lines to state the end of a measure and a double bar line to end the exercise or piece.

If you review the diagram above, you'll notice that this grid system also features several numbers placed on top of the horizontal string lines. The numbers written on any given line represent which fret should be played on that string; if a zero is shown, the string should be played open. *Please note that some tablature may feature finger numbers or classical guitar finger notation placed above the tablature rather than in the grid itself.*

Learning the guitar equates to learning new phrases in the language of music. These new phrases come in many forms such as chord charts, scale charts, sheet music, as well as tablature. These different notations work to do one thing, communicate information.

Tablature is like sheet music with a few distinct differences. For one, tablature, while it relates to the musical staff in the way it designates notes, doesn't actually detail note rhythm as it is written traditionally. Rather, tablature is written to tell the guitarist which frets and which strings to place their fingers on to create chords and melodies, but doesn't typically feature information about rhythm.

Sheet music is an effective means of communicating all aspects of a music to the studying musician. Sheet music tells us which notes will be included within a piece; it provides the rhythm of said piece with a rhythm value for every note. Musicians who play piano, percussion, or wind instruments are often taught to read standard notation, the versatile language of sheet music.

Although learning sheet music is not necessarily a requirement of learning to play the guitar, it can be a useful skill for many styles of music. Some examples include jazz and classical guitar. It also is essential to learn to read standard notation if you were to perform in musical theatre productions or cabaret style shows. In addition, guitarists can also learn music written for other instruments by learning to read sheet music in standard notation, which can be useful in a setting where you may be doubling horn parts, as in a funk or fusion band.

Let's Start Playing Already!

With all of this guitar talk I'm sure you're pining to get your hands on the fretboard. You're probably ready to start wooing audiences with sweet serenades, or just looking forward to learning the arduous G chord. Whatever the case, it's almost time to get playing, but we have to discuss one thing first. The importance of warming up your hands before you play your guitar.

A common problem many guitarists suffer from is called a repetitive motion, or repetitive strain, injury (RMI / RSI). This problem, while it takes some time to develop, is caused by using poor guitar technique over the course of many hours as well as not warming up before you play. Therefore, we need to talk about *how* to warm up before we play, and of course good technique to help prevent injury.

An Essential Warmup Exercise

A great way to warm up and get your fingers moving is to take this exercise and play through it until your hands feel good and warm. This exercise only takes place on the first few frets and, at first, it can seem intimidating. That said, this warm-up exercise is only meant to get your hands loose and relaxed and should be taken slow and deliberate. Give it a try!

Hand Warmup

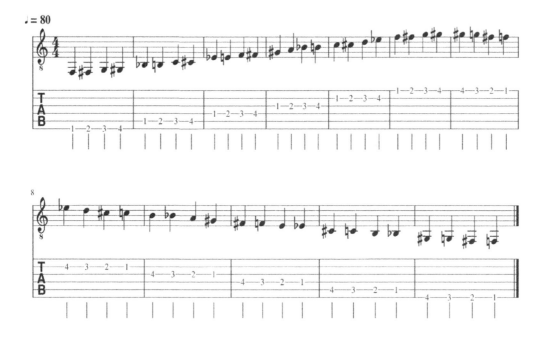

45

Guitar Foundations: Getting Started with Chords

Most of the songs you listen to on a daily basis are riddled with chords. You may not know it, but music from genres like pop, rock, jazz, country; really all genres, wouldn't exist without chords. Even if a genre has no instruments, chords are still implied through the music.

This section will finally get our playing started! We will explain what goes into making a chord and get into a few of the different chord types.

What is a Chord?

Here is the textbook definition.

Chord: Two or more notes played at the same time.

Although, most chords that we encounter in Western music are three or more notes; there are just some exceptions. This definition isn't just for the guitar. Chords can be played on one singular instrument like the guitar or the piano, or they can be played by several instruments all chiming in at the same time. Often the notes of a chord will be distributed through the vast instrumental pallet of an orchestra in classical or film music.

How to Read Chord Charts

Chord charts are a way of teaching and communicating how, and where exactly, a chord is played on the guitar. The diagram below is a map of the different parts of the chord chart.

You'll notice that all of these explanations surround a grid system accompanied by several letters, dots, and numbers. This grid symbolizes the fingerboard with vertical lines representing the strings and horizontal lines representing frets that break the fingerboard into sections.

Sometimes this diagram can be confusing to new guitar players. In order to see it correctly, stand your guitar up, preferably on a guitar stand *(or at least lean it against something!)*, and look at the top of the first fret. See if you can find the nut, where the guitar's neck meets the headstock. The nut is shown in the diagram below with a thick black line.

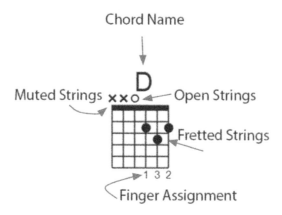

Chord Name

At the top of this chart, you'll find a big letter D. This letter tells us the name of the chord in the diagram, which you can match with any chord chart.

Muted Strings and Open Strings

Along the left and right side of our D chord diagram, below its name, are the terms *muted strings* and *open strings*. These center around two symbols, X's and O's. In a chord diagram, the letter "X" tells us that a string is not played *(or muted, in this context)*. The letter "O" tells us that a string is played *open*, (not fretted). These two symbols are most commonly found in diagrams for *Open Chords*, which we'll learn about shortly.

Fretted Strings

The black dots in this chord chart tell us which frets to press down with our fretting hand, and which string they are fretted upon.

Finger Assignment

As we learn to play the guitar, it's important to understand that each of our fingers has a number much like the strings and frets of the instrument. The finger numbering for both right- and left-handed players is as follows:

Index – 1
Middle – 2
Ring – 3
Pinkie - 4

Along the bottom of each chord chart will be a series of numbers that let us know which fingers will fret which notes. In this case of a D major chord, the fingering would be:

Index Finger (1): 3rd String, 2nd Fret
Middle Finger (2): 1st String, 2nd Fret
Ring Finger (3): 2nd String, 3rd Fret

Detailing each chord in this way is somewhat cumbersome and handled far more efficiently with chord charts.

How to Fret a Note

The most important aspects of fretting notes on the guitar are where you place your finger *between* the metal frets and the amount of finger pressure you apply to each string. As an example, go ahead and test the 3rd fret on the high-E string to find the "sweet spot." You'll find that playing too far away from the fret-center, or on the frets themselves, produces a similar pitch, but an off-sounding, buzzy note. When we play dead-center between the frets, our note remains clear and without the added buzz. This is where you want to aim each of your fretted notes; precisely between the metal frets.

Finger Positioning

One common mistake many beginner guitarists make when first learning chords is attempting to smush all of their fingers onto the fingerboard at once, causing plunky, plinky sounds. Since chords often use most of the fingers on your left hand, this makes sense! These less-desirable sounds often stem from playing notes too close to the metal frets, though, and we want to fix this issue before it becomes a bad habit.

Here are some sure ways to help you avoid this issue: ensure that you are placing your fingers as close to the center of each fret; and make sure your fingers don't lean on, and subsequently mute, strings they shouldn't.

Finger Pressure

Like many guitar techniques, finger pressure is all about balance. When we fret notes on the fingerboard, we want to ensure a level of pressure that will depress the string against the fretboard, but we must avoid applying too much pressure which will needlessly hurt our fingertips, and make our desired pitch go sharp as a result. In addition, too little pressure will result in muted strings; the sound of the notes will be plucky and unclear, similar to the sound produced when playing too close to the frets.

Much like Goldilocks and the three bears' porridge and bedding, we want our finger pressure to be just right; enough pressure to create a clear note, but not so much pressure to hurt our fingers and produce sharp notes.

The First Four Chords: Em, C, D, and G

The first four chords we'll be learning are part of a group known as "open chords". These chords feature both fretted strings and open strings and provide structure to many different songs across different genres.

The sheet music is provided, along with the tablature of each chord. You will notice the music says ♩=80, that means to set your metronome at 80 beats per minute (bpm); alternatively, you could find a drum track on YouTube or in GarageBand at this bpm as well.

Before you Play

As you start to learn these next four chords, keep in mind that the lessons we've learned in our "How to Fret a Note" section still apply here. Be sure each note rings clear when playing each chord. If any note sounds muffled or muted when playing, take the time to play each note individually and allow the notes to ring out; this practice technique is called a *string check*. This helps identify where the odd sounds are coming from in each chord, and which finger to focus on to fix it.

Em – E Minor

First on the list of our first four chords is the *E Minor* chord, or *Em* for short. This chord is almost all open strings, except for two fretted notes with your middle (2nd) and ring (3rd) fingers.

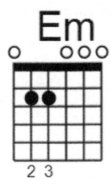

Here is the chord written out in tablature form.

E Minor Chord

Next, we have the *C major* chord or *C* for short. The C-chord uses your first three fingers or your index (1), middle (2), and ring (3) fingers. Please note that the 6th string, our low E ("Eddie" in our acronym) is not played in this chord. As you get more comfortable with this chord, use your ring (3) finger to lightly mute the low E string.

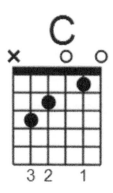

C Major Chord

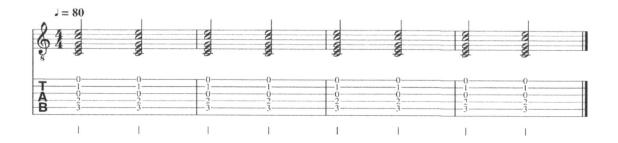

D – D Major

Similar to the C Major chord, D Major uses your index, middle, and ring finger on the "G", "B", and "E" strings (Good-Bye Eddie!), but also includes an open "D" string. If you look closely at the chord chart for the D major chord, you'll also notice a few "X" symbols on the left side of the diagram. Always be sure to avoid playing the thick "E" string and the "A" string when playing the D major chord.

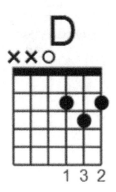

D Major Chord

G – G Major

Out of this list, the G major chord is, hands down, the trickiest. The easiest way to play this chord is to first break it down into smaller pieces. On the high-E string, start by placing your pinkie (4) on the 3rd fret. Try plucking the 1st string with your finger, or your pick. Once you have a solid, clear-sounding note on the high-E string we can continue to your index (1) and middle (2) finger placement. When studying the G major chord diagram, you'll notice that three of the strings (2nd, 3rd, and 4th or the B, G, and D strings) aren't fretted. We can leave those three strings open and move down to the two thickest strings. When playing the "lower" portion of the G major chord, we'll want to first place our index or (1) finger onto the 5th (A) string on the 2nd fret. Following the index, we'll place our second finger on the 6th (low-E) string on the 3rd fret.

Once all three fingers are placed, you should perform a string check; play each string to make sure all the notes are being fretted adequately. Then, celebrate! The G major chord is difficult to play because of all the weird finger stretching and pressing. Unless you're familiar with other stringed instruments, this hand position can feel quite unnatural. While it may feel odd at first, keep at it. The first steps to learning the guitar are all about repetition and reworking until things start to fit together.

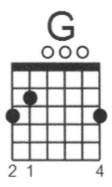

G Major Chord

Chord Changing Exercises

Once you've got the hang of these first few chords, it's time to start playing them together and working toward our first song. This exercise features changes between the E minor chord and the C chord. It starts off playing one strum per *measure*–the space between the black lines on the musical staff–and progresses to two strums per measure, changing between chords throughout the exercise. For right now, don't be concerned with the musical notation above the tablature; we will get into the basics of rhythm and time signatures in detail after we play these chord exercises.

E Minor to C

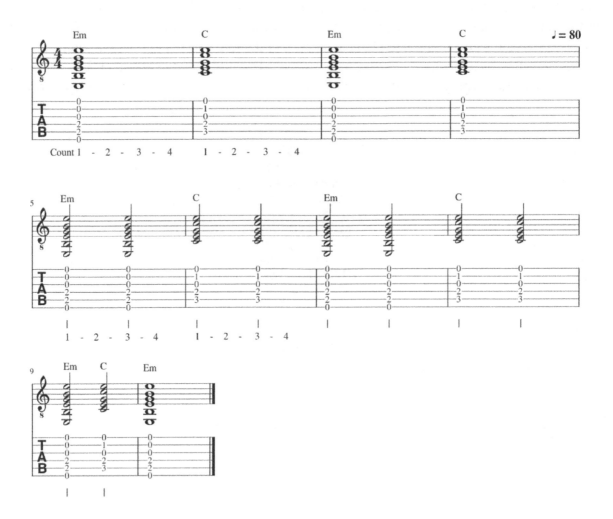

Let's take the C major chord and add a D major chord to the equation, now. This exercise may be a bit challenging to get on the first try, but don't rush it! These exercises are made to be taken slowly and take time to get down properly. It's far more important to make sure the sounds ring out clearly than getting through the exercise as fast as you possibly can.

C Major to D Major

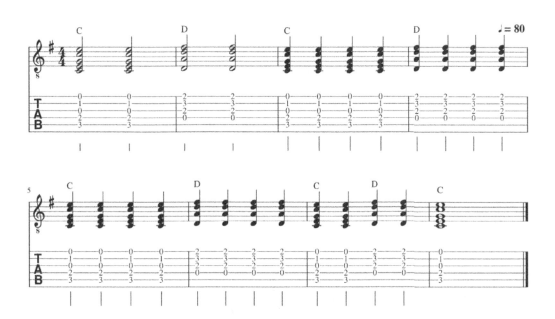

Now that we have a good grasp on the C and D chords, let's spice things up a bit. This next tune adds in the E minor chord for a bit of a sadder sound. Make sure to pay attention as there are a few surprise chord changes placed later in the piece.

New Ground: E Minor

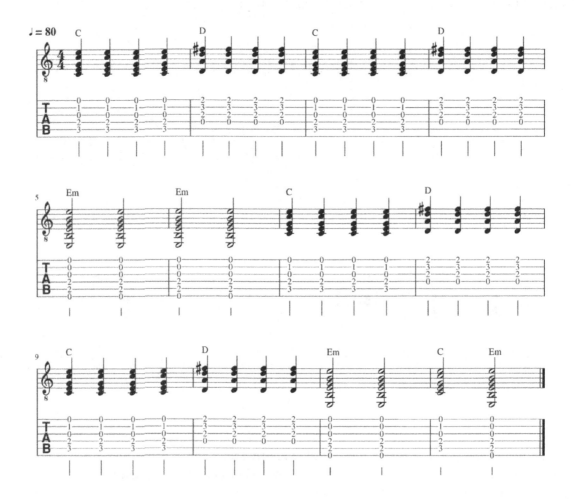

This next piece, "Put It All Together!", takes all of the open chords we've learned so far (Em, G, C, and D) and puts them together in one song. Some of the changes in between these chords may be a bit challenging at first. If the chord changes in this tune are a bit quick for you, please play this piece at any speed that allows you to play the chords, and the notes within them, as clearly as possible; e.g., if you are playing with a click, slow down the bpm when you first attempt this exercise. Go ahead and give it a shot!

Put It All Together!

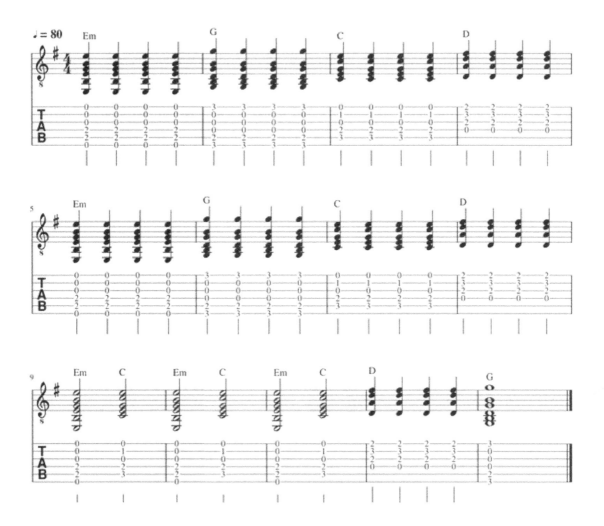

Chords, Their Feeling, and Their Construction

As you play through these first four chords, you might notice that some sound generally happier or sadder when compared to other chords in the same group. Give it a quick test with the G major and E minor chords. Does the G chord sound a little bit more upbeat? Does the E minor chord sound kind of sad?

If it's tough to tell the difference right now, don't sweat it. When we start playing the guitar, identifying the individual notes within chords can be difficult but you'll get it with time.

For now, just remember that major chords tend to have a happier sound and minor chords tend to produce a sadder sound.

But, why is that?

The reason behind the difference in sound between major and minor chords relates to how chords are built.

Chords, including the four we've learned and the chords we'll learn in this guide, are just three or more notes played at the same time. That's right, only three notes.

For example, here are the notes of the four chords you've just learned:

E Minor: E, G, and B
C Major: C, E, and G
D Major: D, F#, and A
G Major: G, B, and D

Only three notes? But we just played six strings for some of these chords! Yep, three notes. The notes of these three-note chords, or *triads*, are repeated across the six strings, producing a fuller sound. Take a look at this G major chord diagram to see where the notes G, B, and D are played on the guitar.

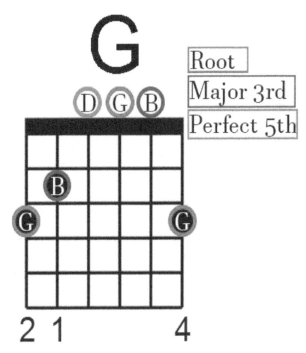

By looking at the G major chord chart, we can see where the first "stack" of three notes in the G major chord appears on the fingerboard. The notes G, B, and D are played on the sixth, fifth and fourth strings. The same notes repeat on the remaining three strings, with the exception of the note D.

Minor chords, although they sound different from major chords, also feature three notes repeated across the six-strings. Let's take a look at the E minor chord chart as an example.

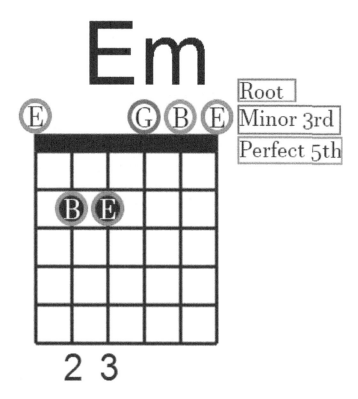

Our E minor chord is built using the notes E, G, and B but this chart seems to be out of order, doesn't it? While the notes don't necessarily line up in an orderly fashion like the G major chord diagram, we can still see how the notes E, G, and B make up our E minor chord.

If we look at the color-coded keys in both of these diagrams, we can immediately see what the difference between a major and a minor chord is.

These keys tell us how the notes of each chord are separated by way of *intervals*; an interval is basically just the distance between two notes. In music, when two notes are played, they are said to be separated by an interval. The distance between E and B can be described with an interval, as can the distance between G and D.

The color-coded keys tell us that both major and minor triads are built using a root note, a note one perfect 5th interval from the root note, and one additional note. The only difference between the two triads is which additional note is played with the root note and the perfect 5th.

Major triads include: a root note, a note one *major* 3rd from the root note, and a note one perfect 5th from the root note.

Minor triads include: a root note, a note one *minor* 3rd from the root note, and a note one perfect 5th from the root note.

Surprisingly, this one little difference is what makes major chords sound happy and minor chords sound sad.

Again, we want to reiterate that the difference in sound between these two chords can be hard to hear for players who've been playing for years, let alone those who are just getting started with the guitar. If the differences aren't quite clear to you yet, don't worry about it. Once your finger strength improves and your calluses are built up, hearing the difference between the chords will be far easier.

Rhythm Basics

If you can shred on the guitar, you'll be a crowd favorite among guitarists. If you can shred with *rhythm*, you'll be a crowd favorite among all listeners.

Rhythm is a topic that all guitarists, and all musicians, need to understand to an intense degree. It's the beat in a song. It's what makes a tune feel controlled, yet powerful. Rhythm is the underlying foundation of a song that makes us feel a certain way when we hear it.

Let's dive in and learn more about how to make our guitar playing sound great just by keeping ourselves in time.

Beat

The term "beat" has a few different meanings depending on who you're talking to. If you ask a friend or family member what *beat* means, they'll probably tell you that it's the part of a song, typically the drums, that people dance or tap their foot to. And they'd technically be right.

But, what if a song doesn't have a drumbeat? What are our strumming and rhythm patterns based on, then?

In cases where songs are played without percussion instruments, it helps to have a stronger definition of the term *beat*.

The beat of a piece of music is a subtle count acknowledged by a musician. In performance and in practice, musicians will often maintain an even count in their head or with their foot to make sure that all of the notes are played with rhythmic order. In pieces that feature percussion, the beat is generally more obvious and pronounced. In songs without drums, the beat is mostly felt.

Bon Jovi's "Livin' on a Prayer" is an excellent example of this pronounced *beat* we're talking about and, as an added bonus, features a ripping guitar solo around the three-minute mark.

The concept of beat is easiest to hear if you pay attention to the drums. Primary beats play the bass drum on beats 1 and 3, and the snare drum on beats 2 and 4.

"Livin' on a Prayer" – Bon Jovi

Tempo

Now that we've established what the beat is in music, it's essential to discuss how tempo affects the speed of a song and the *beat* within it.

Tempo is, in essence, the rate of speed referenced when playing or creating music. The tempo of any song is measured in beats per minute (BPM) and tells us how fast or slow a song is. A rock song like "Ace of Spades" by Motörhead (140 BPM) can be described as using a fast tempo. On the other hand, a song like "Kashmir" by Led Zeppelin (80 BPM) has a slower tempo.

In short, tempo tells us the speed of the beat in any given song or musical line; sometimes a piece of music will have that more subtle beat we discussed before.

Musical Notes and their Meaning

If you've ever looked at a piece of sheet music, or the example songs provided in this guide, you'll notice that each staff is covered in a bunch of solid and hollow black dots and lines. These combinations of black dots and lines provide a detailed roadmap of what notes to play and how long to play each note on a staff.

Each of these symbols has a different musical meaning and tells us how long to hold notes in a piece of sheet music. Take a look at the diagram below, for reference. This is the musical note hierarchy and even if you don't plan to learn to read sheet music in standard notation, it's worth learning the note values if you intend to play with other guitarists or musicians because they will likely use the elements of this diagram in some form to communicate musical ideas.

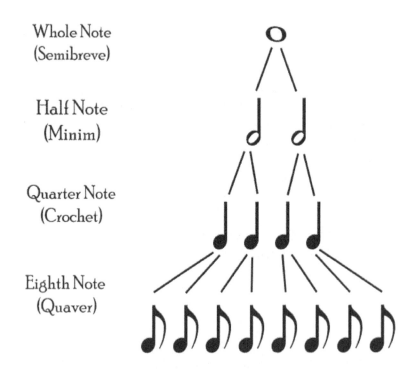

Whole Note
(Semibreve)

Half Note
(Minim)

Quarter Note
(Crochet)

Eighth Note
(Quaver)

Each of these notes

Whole Notes (Semibreve)

One Whole Note = Four Beats

At the top of our rhythm tree is the whole note, or *semibreve* for our friends across the pond, which is the longest note in our example above. This symbol tells us that we're to hold the note for four beats. In terms of guitar playing, playing a whole note means that we would pluck a note and let it ring out for four beats, which we can keep track of by tapping our foot.

Half Note (Minim)

One Half Note = Two Beats

The half note, or *minim*, tells us to play a note for *half* as long as we would when playing a whole note. In other words, while we play a whole note for four beats, we play a half note for two beats; Another way to look at the note values is to relate them to each other. A half note is worth two beats, so we would pluck a string on the guitar and let it ring for 2 of our foot taps.

Quarter Note (Crochet)

One Quarter Note = One Beat

A quarter note, or *crochet*, is equal to one beat (one-quarter of a whole note).

1 - 2 - 3 - 4

Eighth Note (Quaver)

One Eighth Note = ½ Beat

While the rest of the notes we've looked at so far seem to follow a consistent pattern with our 1 – 2 – 3 – 4 count found in music, the eighth note is a bit different. An eighth note, or *quaver*, is one-eighth of a whole note, one-quarter of a half note, and one-half of a quarter note. So, how do we count the eighth note if it doesn't fall in line with our count?

In music, eighth notes feature in-between counts with the word "and", which we notate using an ampersand (&). Let's go back to our original counting example to get a better idea of how this works. With quarter notes, we know that each quarter note is equal to one beat. This means that for each number in *1 – 2 – 3 – 4*, we'd play a quarter note.

Eighth notes are counted with an "and" separating each number in our four-number count: *1 – And – 2 – And – 3 – And – 4 – And*. Written in standard notation, eighth notes look like this:

1 & 2 & 3 & 4 &

Measures

The diagram above consists of several vertical and horizontal lines that, when put together in this way, are referred to as a musical *staff*. This diagram combines both sheet music and tablature notation, both of which feature vertical *bar lines*. These bar lines are used to separate the staff into sections called *measures*.

Measures help musicians identify sections of songs in both standard notation and tablature. These sections determine how long to hold each note or chord based on the *time signature* notation at the beginning of each piece or the different parts in a composition.

The Metronome

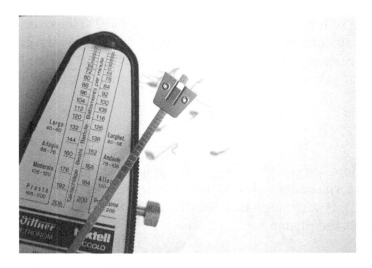

In the previous sections, we've explained quite a bit of information about rhythm and the way rhythm works in a short period of time. We've covered the baselines with beat, tempo, and a few of the different subdivisions of musical notes, but, as beginners, counting notes can still be somewhat difficult. Wouldn't it be easier if something could help us count the beats in a measure while we focus on chord shapes and finger positions?

Fortunately, such a thing exists.

Meet the *metronome*. A simple tool used by instrumentalists and vocalists alike, musicians use the metronome to practice and play exercises and songs. Metronomes are incredibly useful because, once you've selected a tempo, the metronome will tick in time with a musician's preferred BPM and continue ticking until you shut it off. This can be quite helpful in learning the songs and techniques within this guide as most of the songs feature a tempo marker at the beginning of each piece.

However, the metronome is more than just a tempo tracker. It can also be used to give us a benchmark on our performance for a certain piece. When we first learn to play the guitar, even slow songs can seem lightning-fast and out of our reach. We miss beats, fumble over our fingers, and sometimes we even drop our picks inside of our acoustic guitar. It's frustrating.

So, how can we use the metronome to become faster and more deliberate in our chord changes and finger movement?

The answer: play the fast song *slow* with the metronome. Once we know the tempo of a piece or an exercise, we can use the metronome to see how "on-time" we are with the piece or exercise. As important as playing the correct notes is when learning to play the guitar, it's arguably *more* important to play with good timing.

From here onward, we recommend using the metronome with all of the songs placed in this guide to: 1) get a clear idea of how fast the song should play, and 2) adjust the tempo of a piece to a comfortable rate. Again, there is no shame in slowing a piece down to a comfortable rate. Doing so implies that you're treating the guitar as not only a hobby, but a discipline. You can find free metronome apps for any device, or you can go to your local music store and purchase a physical one.

Time Signature

As you begin to explore songs and arrangements, you will likely find an odd (or even) pair of numbers placed before a piece of music in standard notation. This pair, similar looking to a fraction (don't worry, it isn't!), is what musicians refer to as the *time signature* and plays a key role in helping us identify musical rhythm.

In short, time signatures give us information about how many beats fit within each measure within a piece of music. In addition, time signature also tells us what length of time is ascribed to each measure which makes playing "in time" in individual and group cases, far easier.

To understand time signature, we first must acknowledge the two-number "fraction" symbol that dictates time signature in music. Take 4/4 as a quick example:

Each time signature notation consists of two numbers. A top and bottom number or, like math class, a numerator and a denominator.
The *top number* in a time signature tells how high to count in order to get to our number of beats in each measure.

The *bottom number* in our time signature tells us how fast to count these beats.

Meet the most common time signature used in today's music, the "four-four" time signature. 4/4 time is one of the most common time signatures used in rock, pop, country, and blues genres and will likely show up in a large majority of the songs you learn.

4/4

Based on our description of the top and bottom numbers in time signature notation above, we can state that 4/4 means that each measure will equal the value of four quarter notes in length. This means that a measure could consist of one whole note (equal to four beats), two half notes (equal to two beats), four quarter notes (equal to one beat), or eight eighth notes (equal to one half of a beat); not every time signature is this convenient way, *four-four time* is simply what these rhythms are based on. This list of notes could go on forever with variations of each note and their respective length, as well as the many subdivisions of notes that exist, but the point stands that 4/4 implies a specific length of time for each measure in a piece of music.

3/4

Like the discussion of 4/4 time signature, 3/4 time uses the same method to assign each measure with a certain number and kind of note. In the case of 3/4, we know that the top number tells the *quantity* of a specified note, three, and the bottom number tells us which specific note *quality* is related to the top number. In effect, 3/4 tells us that there will be three quarter notes worth of time in each measure; the top number tells us three, the bottom number tells us they are as fast as our quarter notes are.

This time signature is commonly associated with waltzes like Dmitri Shostakovich's "Waltz No. 2". If you take a listen to this piece, you'll notice that the *1 – 2 – 3 – 4* count doesn't exactly work here. This is because each measure in 3/4-time consists of the time value related to three quarter notes or any equivalent divisible value. Therefore, 3/4-time is counted as *1 – 2 – 3, 1 – 2 – 3*.

Taking this example further, we can also acknowledge that a whole note, equal in time value to four quarter notes, will not fit into a measure in 3/4 time because a measure in 3/4-time only has space for three quarter notes. A half note will, as will several quarter and eighth notes. We can get a better idea of what *will* work with measures in 3/4-time by reviewing the diagram below.

In Measure 1, we can see that we're able to fit one half-note and one quarter-note within our defined measure. This is because our time signature dictates that our beat is a quarter note and each measure in 3/4-time is allotted three beats. The half-note is held for two beats and the quarter note is held for one beat, giving us three beats, total.

In Measure 2, we have three notes, all equal to a quarter note. Measure 2 may look different from Measure 3 but all it does is double the notes and splits the available time among them equally. Such is the essence of eighth notes.

Measure 4 combines aspects of Measures 2 and 3 and lists two quarter notes and two eighth notes, giving us our required three beats. We have one beat per quarter note, or two beats, and an additional half-beat per eighth note. Combining these two half beats gives us the final quarter note to complete the measure with three beats.

As we learn to play the guitar, we must do so with the understanding that we are learning with the ultimate goal of playing music. While bedroom shredding or strumming certainly has its (at times, awesome) merits, we, as musicians, should take a look at how the timing of our notes affects our playing. This is an integral part of being a musician, especially when performing with others.

Upstrokes and Downstrokes

G Major Chord

Let's start on the left side and work right. On the leftmost portion of the staff, you'll notice an ornate symbol placed above the vertically-oriented term *TAB*. The symbol on the topmost section of the staff tells us that this is a *treble clef* and tells us which pitches, or notes fall upon or between each line. The groups of notes are used to show what each chord consists of. Above each chord is a symbol representing an upstroke or downstroke for strumming; more details on this in the following page.

The TAB symbol tells us that this is in fact a guitar tab and expresses that each line will act as a single string while numbers across these lines tell us the frets to play on these strings.

In short, both notations explain how to read the music we're playing to varying degrees.
To the right of the *clef* symbol in this arrangement are the numbers "4/4". This notation is used to tell us the time signature.

Each musical piece, tab or otherwise, is broken into smaller sections of notes called *measures*. These measures, which span all Western music genres and styles, serve two functions. 1., they make the piece far easier to read and 2., they play a partial role in identifying how much time each note or chord is held.

Strumming Study: Rhythm and Chords

We have our four basic starter chords, now it's time to make some music! This section will cover several rhythm patterns, upstrokes, downstrokes, and the essentials of most simple songs.

Upstrokes and Downstrokes

Now that we have our fretting hand prepared with some chords, it's time to give some TLC to our forgotten picking hand. To review guitar rhythm playing, it's essential to understand the difference between downstrokes and upstrokes.

Downstrokes: Start with your picking hand positioned *above* the string closest to your face. Guide the pick through the strings in a downward motion while opening your arm.

Upstrokes: Start with your picking hand positioned *below* the string lowest to the ground. Guide the pick through the strings in an upward motion while closing your arm.

As we begin to dive into the different rhythm and strumming patterns, you'll notice that the sheet music we work from details these up and downstrokes with a few symbols.

The *downstroke* or *"down-bow" symbol* looks entirely different from the upstroke symbol. This notation closely resembles a top-heavy rectangle with the bottom side removed.

⊓

The *upstroke symbol* represents a tall "V" with thin upward arms. In musical terms, this is referred to as an "up-bow" symbol.

V

The easiest way to remember these symbols is to think of the opening in each symbol as the direction to strum the guitar strings. If the symbol opens upward, strum up. If the symbol opens downward, strum down. Let's take a look at some sheet music as an example.

Upstrokes and Downstrokes

G Major Chord

Once you've mastered the "upstrokes and downstrokes" in the previous example, ensuring accuracy of the various upstrokes and downstrokes in their respective positions, we can move on to "Strumming Pattern #1" below. This pattern uses alternating upstroke and downstroke strums on quarter-note chords.

This one is a bit trickier than the last: we are constantly changing strumming patterns from downstrokes to upstrokes; we have more than one chord to worry about,

Remember, each quarter note gets one beat in 4/4-time. This, in turn, makes our count *1 - 2 - 3 - 4*, or if we keep the alternating strumming pattern in mind, we could replace the 4-count with *Down - Up - Down - Up*, in each measure. The tempo of this exercise is set to 80bpm (notes where it says ♩=80), but it is wise to start at a slower tempo on the metronome, then add 5 BPM as you get more accurate.

Strumming Pattern #1

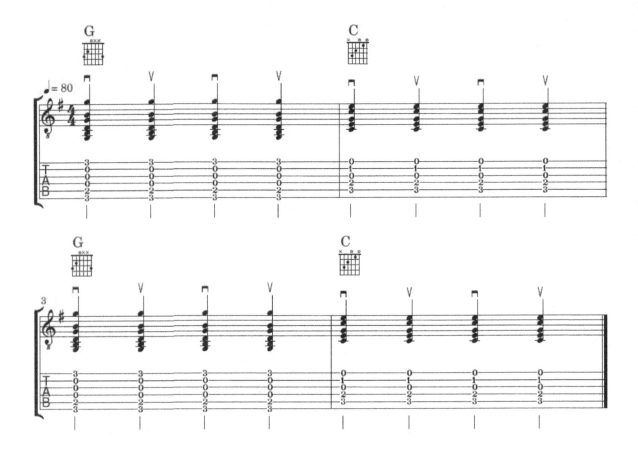

This next pattern, "Strumming Pattern #2" will test your knowledge of quarter notes, half notes, and whole notes on the guitar. As you play through the C and G major chords in this pattern, you might also notice that we've implemented a different bar line than we're used to. This is called the *repeat sign*; it is the double bar line with two dots on the left.

The repeat sign sends us back to the beginning of this exercise. This means that we should play the measures placed before the repeat bar line, and then repeat them once more from the beginning of the song. Because this bar line is positioned before the final G chord, we should only play the last measure *after* playing through the first four measures twice.

Strumming Pattern #2

Down - Up - Down

Our third strumming pattern introduces a combined quarter- and eighth-note rhythm with alternating upstrokes and downstrokes placed throughout the piece. In our usual strumming patterns, we've been strumming on the *1 - 2 - 3 - 4* count, rarely moving away from this pattern. When we talked about quarter notes and eighth notes, we mentioned that a quarter note is equal in time to two eighth notes. Similarly, we also said that an eighth note is equal to one-half of the time a quarter note has.

In our quarter-note count, *1 - 2 - 3 - 4*, we only count the quarter notes. That said, because the quarter note is equal to two eighth notes in time, we can split our quarter note count by two. The resulting count is as follows: *1 - and - 2 - and - 3 - and - 4 - and*. In our strumming pattern exercise, the word "and" is replaced with this ampersand symbol (&). While it may seem kind of silly at first, speaking the counts and rhythms out loud makes learning these patterns far easier. If you don't feel comfortable speaking, clapping the rhythms on your hands or leg works as well.

So, how do we play this exercise?

First, let's see if we can "speak" the rhythm in the first measure by saying the count out loud. We can speak loudly where the notes *are* played and whisper the counts that aren't. Speaking this rhythm would sound something like this - **1**, and, **2**, and, **3**, **and**, **4**, and, - where the bold figures are spoken out loud, and the subscripted "ands" are spoken in your head, or whispered.

Strumming Pattern #3

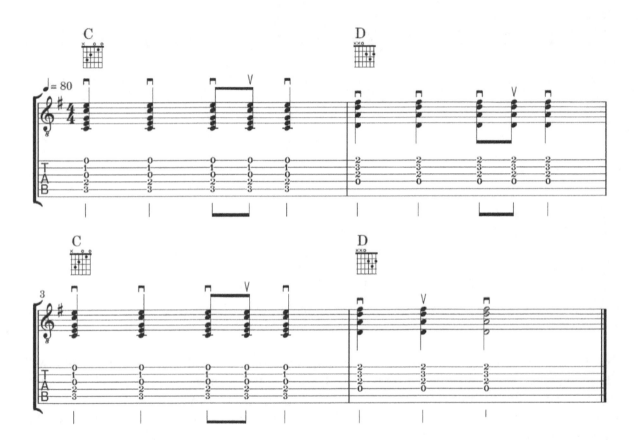

Up next, we have a "Strumming Pattern #4", which *really* moves away from our basic four quarter note count. If you take a look at the rhythm count placed below the first measure, you can see that some of the strums don't fall on the number figures of our rhythm. They actually fall on the "*and*" of the rhythm. This may seem difficult, but rest assured, we'll take care to explain the rhythm.

When we have a rhythm that doesn't line up with our normal count, it is very useful to speak the rhythm out loud while the metronome is playing, like we did in the previous example. We'll use bold figures to indicate which chords are strummed and subscripted figures to indicate which chords aren't strummed in the strumming pattern.

Spoken out loud, the strumming pattern would sound like this: **1**, and, **2, and**, 3, **and, 4, and**. The "and" of one and beat 3 and both in the smaller subscript writing because we don't strum on these beats: the "and" of one is being held out, and there is an eighth rest on beat 3.

Go ahead and set your metronome up and give this strumming pattern a try. Keep in mind that the upstrokes and downstrokes do help play this rhythm but getting the rhythm down should be the main focus in this exercise. Don't forget about the repeat sign!

Strumming Pattern #4

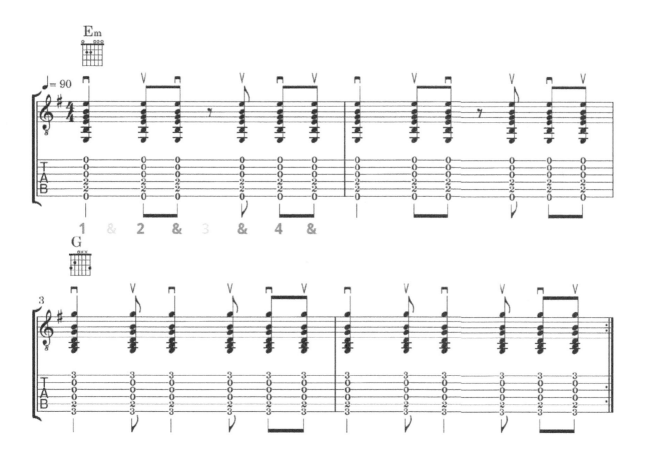

The last exercise in this section, *Quarters and Eighths*, uses the strumming pattern we learned in our third exercise, but adds two extra chords into the mix to take things up a notch. As before, if the strumming pattern gives you trouble, speaking or clapping the rhythm before we play the song can greatly aid in understanding the strumming pattern.

The tempo in *Quarters and Eighths* is set to 90bpm, but please feel free to set your metronome to any tempo, faster or slower, that suits your comfortability with the piece. Playing these exercises can be complicated at first, and it helps to play them at a speed that works for you.

Quarters and Eighths

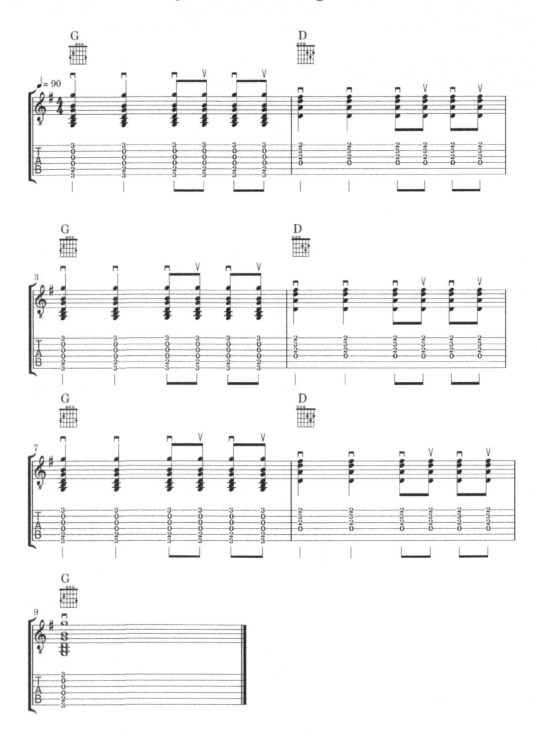

76

Throughout this section we've covered a wide variety of rhythmic topics used in the world of guitar. We've added a variety of strumming patterns to our guitar repertoire as well as added some unique variations of upstrokes and downstrokes to our musical toolbox. In the next section, we'll dive deeper into the expansive realm of guitar chords by learning the next set of open guitar chords.

More Open Chords!

Now that we've learned the four starting chords all guitarists need to know, it's time to up the ante. Next, we'll take a look at the A major, A minor, D minor, and E major open chords.

A - A Major

The open-A major chord falls entirely on the 2nd fret in standard tuning, and as shown in the chord diagram below it uses two open strings. It is important to note that although the low-E string technically "fits" within this chord's structure, it is not traditionally played in this chord shape, hence the "**X**" over the low-E string in the diagram.

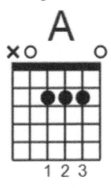

The A Major Chord

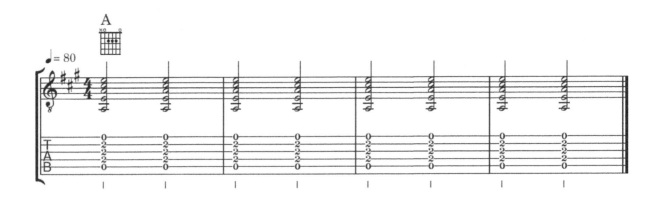

78

A minor is one of the most common chords you'll see as you start to learn the guitar. This chord uses your first three fingers and, like the A major chord, does not include the sixth string when played.

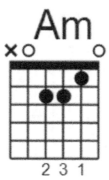

The A Minor Chord

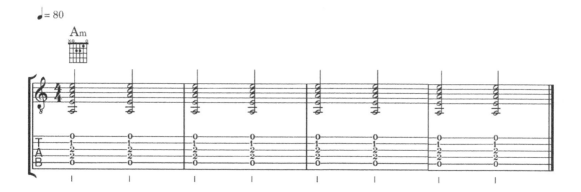

Dm - D Minor

D minor is closely related to the D major chord. Both of these shapes are quite similar but with only one subtle difference. The difference is your 1st finger will play the 1st fret on the high-E string rather than the 2nd fret.

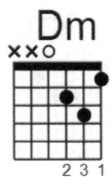

The D Minor Chord

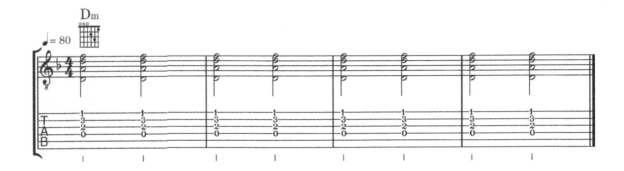

E major, like the rest of these chords, is quite similar to its minor counterpart. This chord requires all six strings to be strummed when played and uses your first three fingers to achieve the proper E major sound.

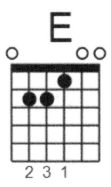

The E Major Chord

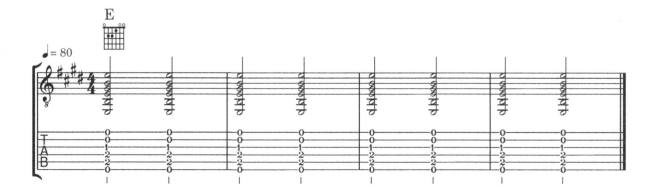

F Major (Mini Version)

Now that we have a good grasp on our open chords, it's time to take a look at chords that take a bit of a different path on the fingerboard. In the next chapter we will get into barre (said *bar*) chords extensively, but let's start with an appetizer of a barre chord, one that's a little less high maintenance. The first on the list, F major, is quite difficult to play and falls into the *barre chord* family. If you look at the chord chart below, you'll notice that this chord doesn't use any open strings and uses your index finger to fret two notes at one time. This takes place on the 1st fret and should be practiced slowly to ensure proper technique.

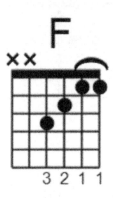

The F Major Chord

mini barre

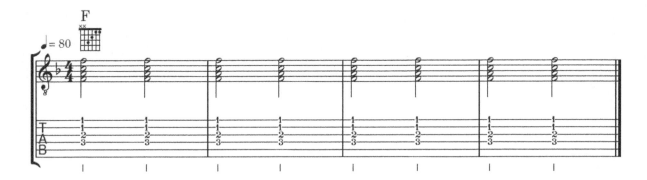

Barre Chords - Index Finger Intensive ... Sort of

Barre chords are a common point of mass frustration for many novice guitar players. Unlike open chords, barre chords are fretted on five or six strings at a time. The main stopping point for most guitarists is the use of one finger (your index finger) to span the width of a single fret, covering five or six strings simultaneously. It can be difficult to make these shapes when you first learn them, but it's important to keep pressing onward. These shapes become far easier as you practice them and will expand your playing from the first three frets to the entire fingerboard.

This next section will provide all the information you need to know to learn barre chords and build upon your guitar knowledge. Let's get started!

As we take a closer look at barre chords, understanding how the root notes of barre chords becomes increasingly important. Understanding the root notes of these chords allows you to take your growing knowledge of chord construction and apply it to the rest of the fingerboard.

The Four Basic Barre Shapes

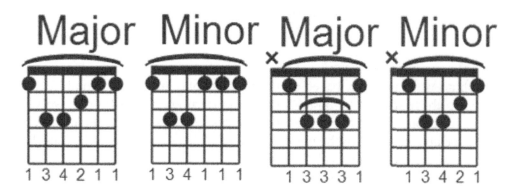

The basic barre chord shapes we'll be learning include four chords in total, with a major and minor shape beginning on both the sixth and fifth strings.

The chords below are a major and a minor chord shape. Note the red circles on the left side of both images. This establishes the root note of both chords. You may also notice that the chords don't list any chord information aside from "Major" and "Minor" at the top of each diagram. The reason for this is that these two chords shapes will be either major or minor, regardless of where you play them on the fingerboard.

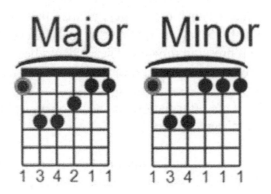

Now that we have a good grasp on the chord shapes, it's now more important to pay close attention to the *root* or *tonic* note given by the red circle in these diagrams. We'll be applying this concept to the fingerboard and work to understand what this note means in relation to the frets we play them on.

The fingerboard diagram below details the notes on the bottom two strings. This gives us a better idea of what chord we're playing, based on the frets we play it on. For example, if we take the major barre shape above and play it on the sixth string starting on the fifth fret, we've effectively played an A major chord. If we take this example further and switch out the major chord for the minor chord shape above, we'll still be playing a chord with an "A" note in the root, but the chord will be minor because of the shape we've chosen.

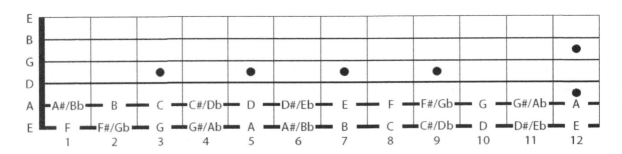

Sixth String Barre Chords

Let's take a look at a few examples of barre chords with a root or tonic note on the sixth string (low E string).

Major

The three chords in this section, F, G, and A major, all use the same basic shape we discussed at the beginning of this section. All of these chords use your index finger to provide a baseline for the rest of the chord, with your ring, pinkie, and middle fingers following closely behind. As you start to learn these chord shapes, it's key to understand that just because your index finger provides the baseline of these shapes, it should not be pressing down all six strings at one time.

In contrast, your index finger on your fretting hand should *cover* the six strings, but place an emphasis on pressing down the sixth, second, and first strings; this helps your finger maintain a more ergonomic shape. If you look at the diagrams below, you'll notice that your ring, pinkie, and middle fingers take care of fretting the fifth, fourth, and third strings respectively. This should save your index finger from extra strain and make these chords, although they are difficult at first, far easier to play.

Lastly, please note that the G and A major barre chords are the first chords we'll play that aren't played right up next to the nut of the guitar, and start to move us toward the body of the guitar. Take G major, for example. The diagram shows that this chord actually starts on the third fret of the guitar even though the thick guitar nut line is still visible in the diagram. In the case of A major, the fingerboard marker, "5fr," tells us that the chord starts on the fifth fret, with the sixth through ninth frets following the starting position.

Go ahead and give these a try. The F major barre chord is easily the most difficult to play out of these three and it's more than okay to skip to the G major and A major chords for the time being.

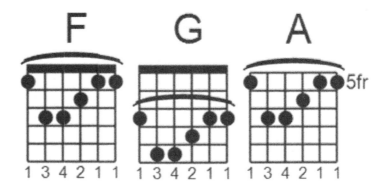

⇦Remember to take note of the new 5th fret position for the A Major chord diagram!

85

Major Barre Chords - F, G, and A

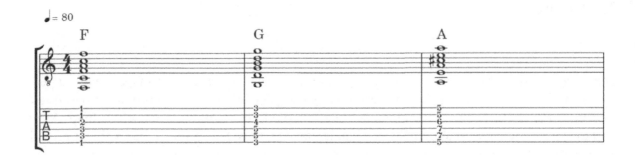

Minor

Minor barre chords are slightly harder than major barre chords for one simple reason: your index finger has one more string to hold down, the G string. Otherwise, maintain the same good hand position and pressure that you did for the major chords. Here are the same chords as our last example, but the chords are minor instead of major.

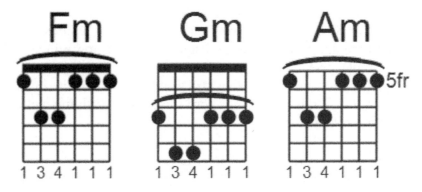

Minor Barre Chords - F, G, and A

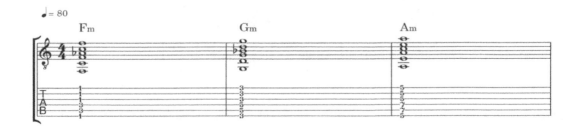

These are just a few examples of what the major and minor barre chords look like on the sixth string. These major and minor barre chord shapes can be played anywhere along the sixth string and will produce different chords depending on which fret you play them on. Go ahead and experiment with these. They take some time to get down but using the two charts featuring highlighted root notes with the notes of the fifth and sixth strings will amplify your guitar playing.

Sixth-String Barre Chord Exercises

Transitioning between various barre chord shapes can be somewhat difficult to get used to. To help you cement these shapes into both your hands and your minds, we've placed several chord changing exercises in this next section. These exercises vary in tempo, note duration, as well as the chords used. As you practice these exercises, you may be tempted to increase the speed of the song. We welcome you to do so, but we'd also like to make clear the difference between practicing these exercises and playing them.

Practicing these songs means to make sure each note rings out clearly within each chord as the piece progresses. Pay attention to appropriate finger pressure and please, PLEASE, don't be dismayed by mistakes. If you notice that the song's speed seems to give you difficulty, knock the metronome back a few BPM, and just slow it down. The goal here is not song memorization, but learning how the chords feel and gaining a fundamental familiarity to new areas of muscle memory.

Soft Landing – Using the F, A minor, and G Barre Chords

Soft Landing

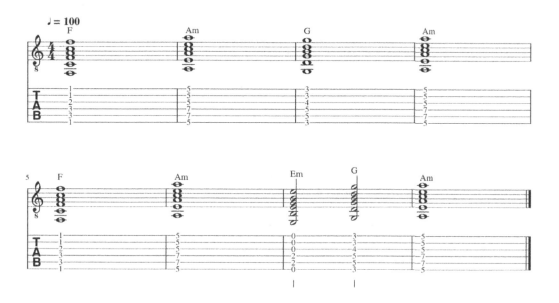

Rainy Day – Practice Notes

Although this song features similar chords to that of the previous exercise, "Soft Landing", it's useful to note that there is no tempo detailed in this song. One aspect of learning to play the guitar is understanding the limit of your ability. The tempo in this piece was omitted for this reason. Take a quick look at this exercise and try it out at a tempo that feels comfortable for you. That tempo could be 100BPM or even 170BPM.

Whether you decide to play this piece in a rapid-fire manner, or at a methodical pace, be sure to keep chord clarity in mind while playing.

Rainy Day

Switch it Up – Practice Notes

Switch it Up is easily the most difficult of these three barre chord exercises. It requires a fair understanding of rhythm, comfortability with open chords, and a fair amount of ability from your picking hand. Although the noted rhythm states that this piece is to be played at 80 BPM, we encourage you to slow down or speed up the tempo in any manner you're most comfortable with.

Like all of the exercises listed in the book, they are not meant to push you to play faster. Although that is a benefit of diligently learning the material and practicing the exercises, the main focus of your practice should be absorbing the material in order to use it at your leisure. This means focusing on not only chord shapes, but also playing them in time. Give this one a shot!

Switch It Up

Fifth-String Barre Chords

Similar to the discussion of sixth-string barre chords above, the two fifth-string (A string) barre chords we'll be learning can be played anywhere along the fingerboard. We've highlighted the root, or tonic notes, in the diagrams below just like the sixth-string barre chords. These highlighted notes indicate the root or tonic of each chord and tell us what the name of each chord is, while the chord's other notes determine whether the chord is major or minor.

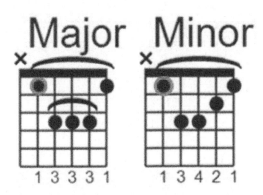

Let's take a look at a few major and minor barre chords starting on the fifth string.

Major

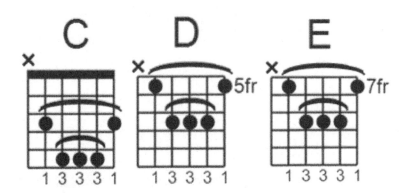

Barre Chords - C, D, and E Major

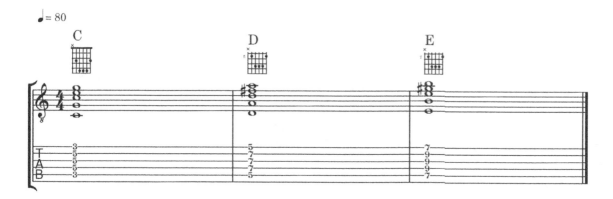

Minor

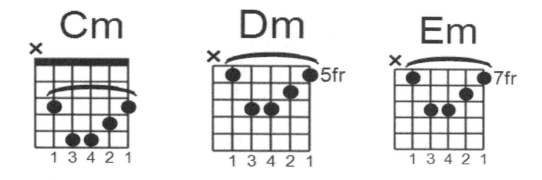

Minor Barre Chords - C, D, and E

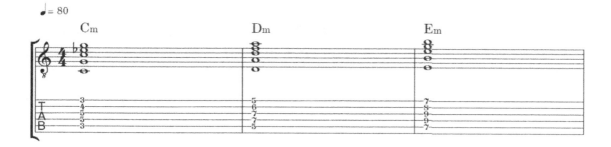

Similar to our sixth-string barre chord discussion, these three examples are just that: examples. This is not to say that the chords given here are the *only* fifth-string barre chords. On the contrary, there are 24 different chords to play between the 1st and 12th frets on the A-string if we're only talking about major and minor shapes. That said, learning these shapes does require consistent review of the *notes of the fingerboard* charts detailed throughout this book.

91

Power Chords

Now that we have a good understanding of how barre chords work and where they get their names from, it's time to dive into the legendary *power chords*. To start, let's talk about what a power chord is.

Based on our introduction to barre chords, we know that each barre chord derives its name from the root note found within each barre chord. In the case of a G major barre chord, the root note "G" comes from the combination of the sixth string (low-E) played on the 3rd fret. If this isn't ringing clear go ahead and take a look at this diagram. If we follow the bottom line of this chart from left to right and count to the 3rd fret, we can see the letter hovering above the line is "G". This will always be the case in standard tuning and will provide the root note for all sixth-string major and minor barre chords.

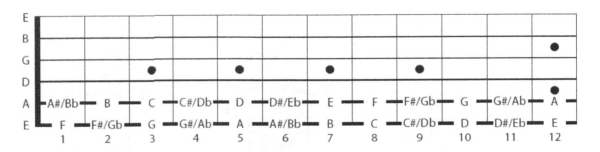

The same idea remains in the case of power chords, although the shape is somewhat different from barre chords. Power chords are composed of the bottom three notes of each major and minor barre chord shape that we've learned. We'll place a few examples here for comparison; the fingers you should use for power chords are your index, ring, and pinky fingers.

Sixth-String Major – From Barre to Power Chord

Here we have the G major barre chord and the G power chord, which can also be called G5. This power chord shape takes the same starting shape from the G major barre chord and uses the sixth, fifth, and fourth strings to make up this three-finger shape.

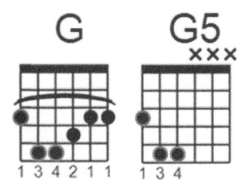

The G Power Chord

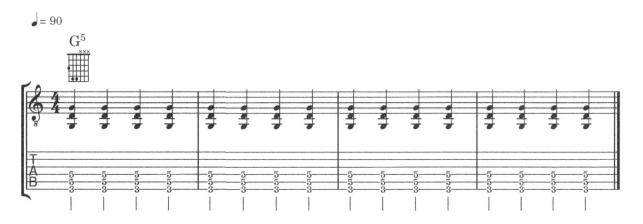

Sixth-String Minor – From Barre to Power Chord

Now take a look at the G *minor* barre chord and notice what happens when we transition to the resulting power chord. We end up with the same power chord as above, the G5 power chord. Why is that?

The reason behind this is that a power chord, although our examples use three finger placements, only requires two notes to be classified as a power chord; the root and the fifth, G and D in this case. As long the root note is played, like we've discussed above with our barre chord examples, and the perfect fifth of said root is played as well, the result will be a power chord.

That lends itself to the question, "How can there only be two notes if three fingers are placed?" The reason that we place three fingers instead of only two is because it adds depth to the chord when the root note is played one octave above the original root note; this is the note on the 5th fret of the D string, which is the note G.

One of the most interesting aspects of the power chord is its ability to stand in place of any major or minor chord. This is because the power chord, for all of its use in modern rock and blues music, isn't inherently major *or* minor. It's an adaptive chord and can be used in place of major and minor barre chords when needed, although it is a good idea to keep barre chords in your guitar arsenal as they provide a fuller sound than traditional power chords.

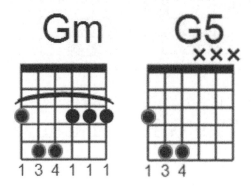

Let's take a look at another example like the F power chord as it relates to the F major and minor barre chords.

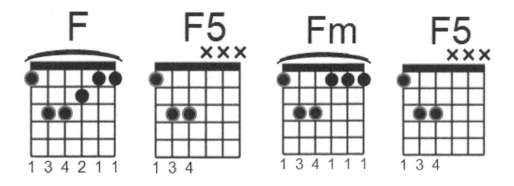

The F Power Chord

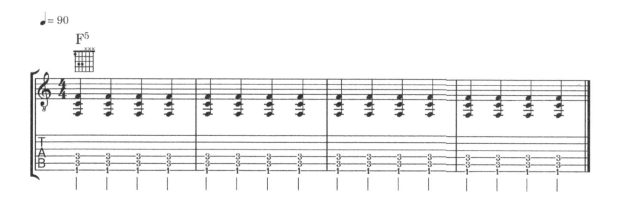

Just as we've described with our G5 power chord in our previous example, the F major and minor barre chords can be broken into the F5 power chord in the same way. As you can see in our diagrams, the highlighted finger positions in our major and minor barre chords are exactly the same as our power chords in the case of our example root note, "F".

The point is that each sixth-string barre chord, major or minor, shares the shape with its relative power chord. Go ahead and try this out along the guitar neck and use the fretboard labels above to see where each power chord can be played along the neck!

Rather than break down each barre-to-power chord relationship, we've placed several different power chord charts here for your study. Be sure to take note of each location as our next song will feature quite a few of these shapes!

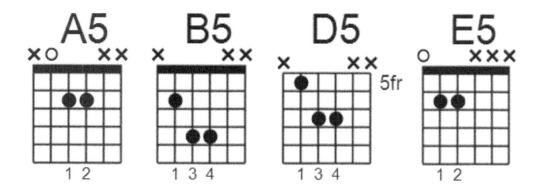

As you can see in these chord charts, the two shapes (power and barre) are quite similar to each other and follow the overall barre shape. One thing that you may have noticed with these power chord shapes is the way they're named. "Chord Name '5'". The '5' actually refers to the way that the power chord is made from scale degrees. The reasoning for the 5 comes from the use of the 5th scale degree in a power chord. In each power chord shape, the ring finger will be responsible for playing a 5th in any scale degree.

We will dive deeper into these concepts in a later section. For now, just know that a power chord features a root note, the 5th scale degree related to said root note, and an octave of the root note starting our chord.

We've placed a quick tune below that describes how the C5, G5, D5, and F5 power chords are written in standard notation as well as tablature. Grab your metronome and give it a try!

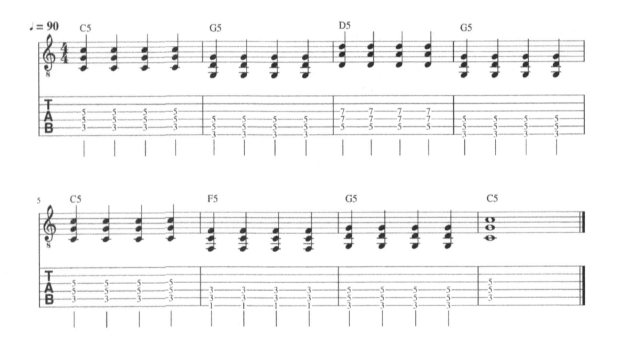

As a final point on power chords, it's important to return to our original discussion on what makes a power chord a power chord. As we discussed previously, a power chord is made up of two parts, a root note, and a relative fifth according to the root note of the chord. With that said, a power chord is not *always* three notes played together.

If you peruse our previous examples of power chords that feature three notes played together, you'll find that the chords have notes on three different strings. Because a power chord only requires two notes (root and fifth), we can also play power chords with just two strings. In this case, we'd be playing what is called an *interval*, or two notes played at the same time. Take a look at this recreation of our previous example song for reference.

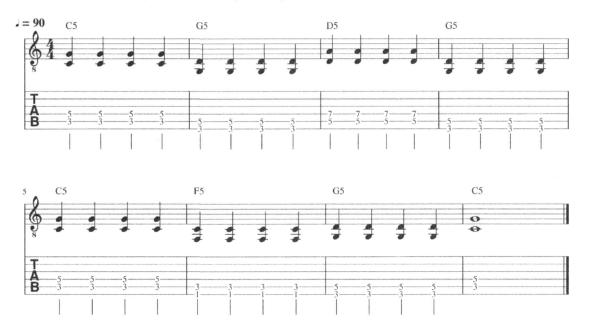

When we review this song and compare it to our previous example, we can easily see that the chords are all nearly identical to each other. The chords are all in the same position along the staff, and they still occupy the same notes within our tablature. With that said, we can also tell that we're missing something: the octave on each of our power chords!

As we discussed when we started, a power chord only needs a root and a relative fifth to be deemed a power chord. Because all of our "chords" in the second iteration of our power chord example fall into this category, they're still considered power chords.

Popular Songs with Power Chords

Because the power chord is such a simple, yet effective tool, many artists use them as the building blocks to create songs in many different genres. Here's a list of several different power chord-heavy songs to check out and learn from.

"Smells Like Teen Spirit" – Nirvana
"Blitzkrieg Bop" – The Ramones
"Godzilla" – Blue Oyster Cult
"Hit Me with Your Best Shot" – Pat Benatar

"Iron Man" – Black Sabbath
"Paranoid" – Black Sabbath
"Enter Sandman" – Metallica

At this point, we've covered quite a bit of material. Open chords, major chords, minor chords, barre chords, power chords, it's a lot to take in. With that said, it's always important to view every practice session, including every new chord and rhythm pattern learned, as a victory!

Seventh Chords

Now that we've covered the vast majority of "starter" chords, it's time to take on something a bit more complex. The *seventh*, or *7ᵗʰ*, chord is commonly used in genres that require a more dedicated knowledge of the inner-workings of music. These genres include jazz, blues, funk, R&B, and also crossover genres like jazz-fusion and progressive rock. That isn't to say there isn't any overlap into genres like country, pop, and rock, there certainly is. Though, the previously mentioned genres use the seventh chord far more often than any other genres or subgenres in music.

So, what is a seventh chord?

In technical terms, a seventh chord is built with three notes, like our other shapes, and features an added fourth note. The term *seventh* in seventh chord refers to the inclusion of the seventh scale degree as the fourth note within our chord. Our open chords and barre chords from earlier contain three separate notes, hence their name "triads". The scale degrees in these chords are root, 3ʳᵈ, and 5ᵗʰ.

In a conversational sense, a seventh chord is a chord with a different tonal quality when compared to the major and minor chords we've learned previously. The seventh chord offers a bit more play in terms of tension and resolution. The seventh chord can also be considered as "uglier-sounding" than our other chords, although this statement is entirely subjective.

The Types of Seventh Chords

Dominant Seventh Chords: Open Positions

The open dominant seventh chords are a must-have for guitar players seeking a little spice in their play. They break out from the stagnant major and minor chords and evoke variety with tension depending on when they're played. More importantly, if you're seeking out chord charts or tabs to your favorite songs, you will eventually come across the unfamiliar seventh chords. Let's have a look at these shapes and make sure you have the tools to tackle such tasks.

For the sake of brevity, we will refer to all dominant seventh chords with a superscripted "7" from here onward.

The Open E^7 Chord

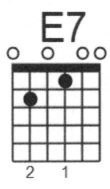

E7, central to blues, country, and rock genres is a dominant seventh chord in the open position. If you refer back to our discussion of the open-string chords, you may find some striking similarities between this seventh chord and our E major chord. Here's a glimpse back through our studies.

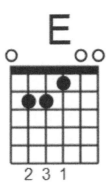

You may notice that the only difference is that our seventh chord is missing a note from the D-string in our E major chord. This is what gives our chord the "7" in E dominant seventh. Let's take a closer look at the differences in tablature form.

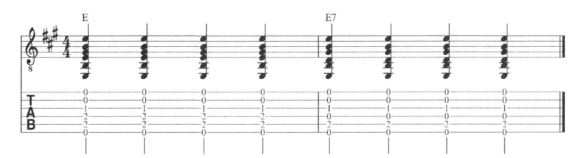

Without getting into complex music theory, the difference between these two chords only lies in the fact that this chord uses an additional note, D, to produce the chord. This occurs when we remove our ring finger from the 2nd fret of the fourth string, giving us the "seventh" in our seventh chord.

Songs that use the E^7 chord:
"Folsom Prison Blues" – Johnny Cash
"Hey Joe" – Jimi Hendrix

The Open A^7 Chord

The open A^7 chord, like the E^7 chord, is similar to its three-note relative, A major. Take a look at the two charts to compare.

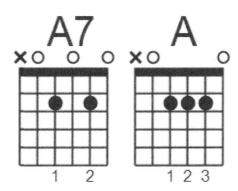

Like the E^7 chord, A^7 removes only one finger from the chord to become a seventh chord. When we do so, we change the note of the third string from an A note to a G note, providing our 7th in the A^7 chord.

Songs that use the A^7 chord:
"Nobody Knows You When You're Down and Out" – Scrapper Blackwell
"Only Love Can Break Your Heart" – Neil Young
"Harvest Moon" – Neil Young

The Open D^7 Chord

In the case of D^7, we only need to flip the chord around to create a dominant seventh chord. Take a look at these chord diagrams to see the difference.

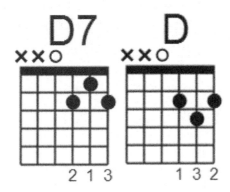

If you look at where the fingers are positioned in the diagram, you can see that we only need to adjust the note played on the B-string to complete our D^7 chord. We simply move our fingers around a bit to play the first fret on the B-string instead of the third fret on the B-string; the fingers that were "up front" are now "in back", and vice versa.

In a moment we will take a look at how these chords can be used in the song "Seventh Chord Changes Blues". This tune features a bar line called an *end-repeat bar-line* in the last few measures of the song. This is the same symbol we had earlier in the book which means, if you recall, to repeat to the beginning of the song.

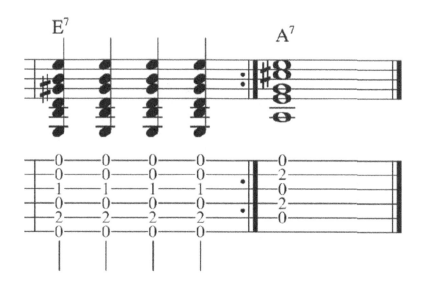

The end-repeat bar-line indicates that everything before this line should be repeated once more before we end the song on the measure *following* the end-repeat bar-line. In addition, this piece does have a few rapid changes throughout the piece so be sure to choose a tempo that allows you to play comfortably with all of the notes within each chord ringing out clearly.

Seventh Chord Changes Blues

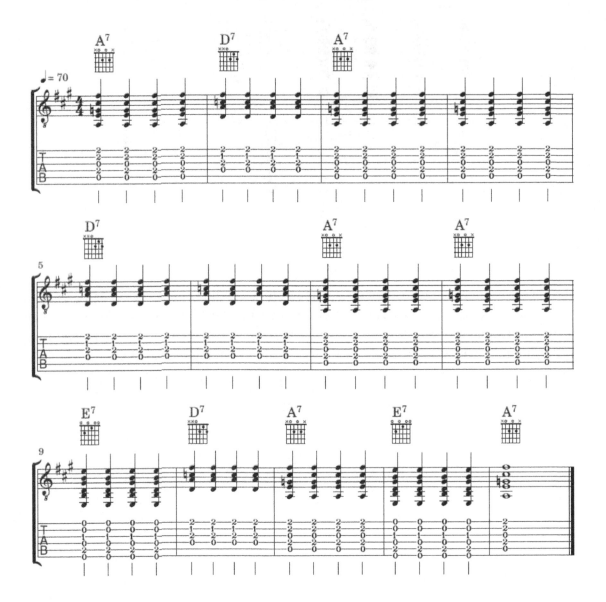

The Open G⁷ Chord

The G dominant seventh chord also features similarities to its major chord relative, and also looks a lot like our C major chord. It's important that we don't get these two chords confused as the sounds of the chords, and the notes within them, are quite different.

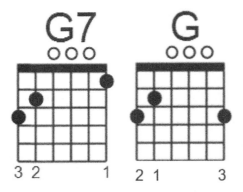

Songs that use the G^7 chord:

"Fire and Rain" – James Taylor

"Can't Buy Me Love" – The Beatles

"The Girl from Ipanema" – Frank Sinatra

The Open B^7 Chord

Out of all of these open-dominant seventh chords, B^7 features the fewest open strings in this section. This chord is played on the top 5 strings with the B string left unfretted.

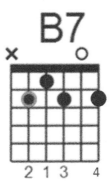

Although this shape seems somewhat plain, it is a surprisingly useful chord shape to memorize. This shape is actually similar to our fifth- and sixth-string barre chords with root notes in the base of the chord. If you take a quick look at the diagram again, you'll notice that the root of this B dominant seventh chord is highlighted in red. Just like our barre chords with roots in the base of the chord, this chord shape can be moved around the fingerboard, creating a variety of seventh chords with one simple shape.

105

Take the D^7 chord for example. This shape can be played in our original position next to the nut, or we can play it on the 5th fret in a more compact shape. Have a look at these diagrams to see what we mean.

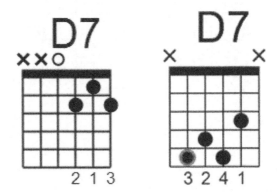

When we use the shape of the B^7 chord and move it to the 5th fret on the A-string, we have a D^7 chord. As another example, let's take a look at the same shape played on the 4th fret of the A-String.

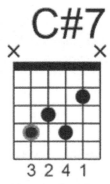

This shape is great because, like our other barre chords, we can move it around the fingerboard to play chords without open strings. This is especially useful when playing in keys that have more than a few spare sharps and flats.

Songs that use the B^7 chord:
"I Walk the Line" – Johnny Cash
"I Guess That's Why They Call It the Blues" – Elton John

Learning these chord shapes and committing them to memory takes time. Be sure to practice these chord shapes as they may come up in later sections.

Minor Seventh Chords: Open Positions

If you're seeking variety in your playing or songwriting, the minor seventh chord offers a rising tension that other chords just can't touch. Learning these chords and keeping them in your "guitar toolbox" allows you to create music that doesn't stick to stagnant major and minor chords.

Minor seventh chords are identified by standard note names like A, F#, or B, followed by a lowercase "m" and normal or superscripted seven in the chord name. Similar to the other chords we've learned, the letter specified in a chord name refers to the chord's root note. It's also common to use the hyphen or dash symbol "-" to imply a minor quality for a chord.

Without any further ado, let's get started on our minor seventh chords in open positions.

The Am^7 Chord in Open Position

The Am^7 chord is played on the first two frets on the guitar and only uses two fingers to play the chord. To start, we can look at the Am^7 chord as a variation on the A minor chord. Let's take a look at the charts.

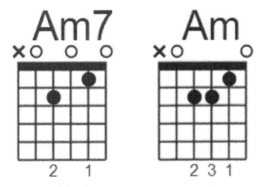

Notice how the only difference between these two chords lies in how we use the third or G-string on the guitar. In A minor, we fret the G string on the second fret. Am^7 uses the open G-string to create the seventh in the title *minor seventh* chord.

Songs that use the Am^7 chord:
"Old Man" – Neil Young
"More than Words" – Extreme
"Stuck in the Middle with You" – Stealers Wheel
The Em^7 Chord in Open Position

Possibly the simplest chord one can play on the guitar, the Em[7] chord is laughably easy to play. It requires one, just one, finger to play the 2nd fret on the fifth string and is essentially the "ol'-reliable" of the minor seventh chords in open position.

Like the Am[7] chord, the Em[7] chord features stark similarities to the E minor chord, with the only difference being the open D-string.

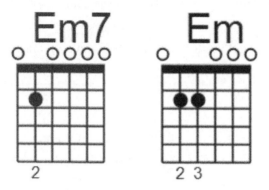

Songs that use the Em[7] chord:
"Yesterday" – The Beatles
"Who Says" – John Mayer

This next song, "Waltzin' Seventh Chords", combines the Am[7] and Em[7] chords in a 3/4-time, and uses a waltz pattern; you may recognize this style from old ballroom dancing where the music, essentially, sounds like it goes "down, up-up" over and over. This is an oversimplification, and no disrespect to classical waltz music, but hopefully it helps for our purposes here.

In our previous songs, we've used quarter and half-note strums of the chords provided in the sheet music, with little difference in rhythm throughout the piece. This tune differs from our previous pieces in that we play one minor seventh chord in each measure, splitting the *1 - 2 - 3* count of 3/4-time with a mix of single-note plucks and chord strums within each measure. The singular notes played at the beginning of each measure are still part of the chord detailed within and above the staff but they're played separately to add rhythmic variety to the piece. Again, be aware that this song is in 3/4-time and that each measure will be counted as *1 – 2 – 3, 1 – 2 – 3*, rather than our usual *1 – 2 – 3 – 4, 1 – 2 – 3 – 4* count.

Waltzin' Seventh Chords

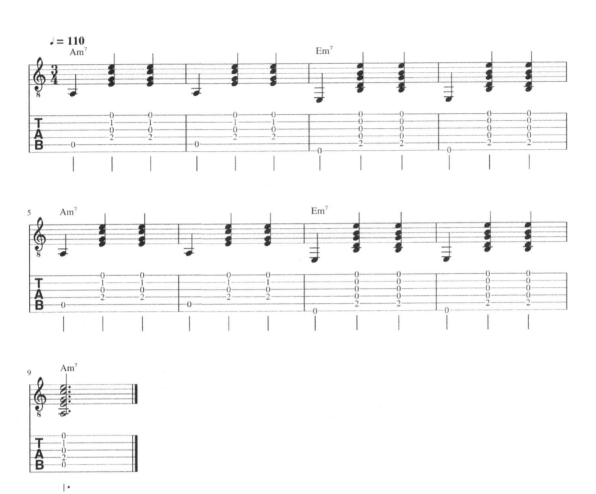

Scales: An Introduction

Have you ever wondered how guitarists create such powerful solos and melody lines? During their solos, professional guitarists seem to pull these ideas out of thin air and produce masterful lines loaded with anticipation and energy. How do they do it?

The answer, in short, is with scales and scale patterns.

Scales break up the twelve possible notes across several octaves in Western music and allow musicians to garnish their music with feeling, emotion, and for some guitarists, face-melting shred fests. They're the basis of all music and provide interest in color and variation across all genres.

This section will list a few of the different scale types, explain what it takes to produce these scales, and teach you how to use them effectively in writing your own solos and songs.

What is a Scale?

In music, a scale is any series of ordered notes in an ascending or descending pattern. Because the western music system is based on a series of equally separated notes, musical scale patterns can be repeated throughout several octaves, which we'll see as we apply these patterns to the fingerboard. In some cases, only playing the notes C, D, and E would meet the definition of a scale.

How are Scales Made?

When we talk about building scales in our guitar study, what we're actually doing is discussing a series of interval patterns inherent within most aspects of music. Consider our previous study of chord diagrams as an example. Throughout our study of chords in this guide, we've acknowledged that a chord consists of three or more notes played at the same time. Although we're aware of the fact that we're playing these notes, we don't necessarily need to know *all* of the notes we're playing. Could you imagine having to think about the notes for every single chord you played? It'd be exhausting!

The reason we're able to play all of these chords without knowing all of the notes within them is because we understand the shape or *pattern* of any given chord. Building and learning scales works in the same way.

Similar to the chords we've learned, scales all start with a *tonic* or *root* note. The tonic of a scale gives us a sound foundation to build the rest of our scale. Once we have our root note, all we need to do is add intervals of *whole steps* and *half steps* to produce a useful scale with patterns.

Whole steps, half steps? What?

Although we haven't covered these terms yet, we've been using whole steps and half steps in different ways throughout this entire guide. We used them in the songs "Twinkle, Twinkle Little Star", "Jingle Bells", and we even made subtle use of whole steps and half steps in our chord changing exercises. Basically, half steps and whole steps are like intervals; they are just words that represent distance traveled in music from one note to the next.

So, what are half steps and whole steps?

Half Steps (H) are defined as one-note step from any starting note position. If we take the note C, for example (3rd fret, A string if you'd like to play along), and add one half step to it, we land on a C-Sharp (C#). Put another way, if you play a note on one fret then play a note one fret higher on the same string, the difference between those two notes is a half step.

Half Steps: Original note plus or minus one fret = Half-Step

Whole Steps (W) are defined as two-note steps from any starting position. If we take the note C again, for example, and add one whole step to it, we're left with a D-note. If we start on one fret and play a note two frets higher on the same string, the difference between the notes is a whole-step.

Whole Steps: Original note plus or minus two frets = Whole-Step

The diagram below provides a visual representation of the difference between half steps and whole steps. A half step is denoted by the solid blue line and the whole-step is given by the solid red line.

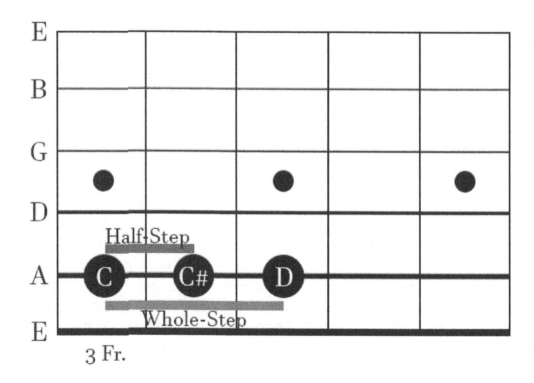

Take the *chromatic* scale, for example. The chromatic scale is built by selecting a starting note, such as C, and adding notes in half steps until we come back around to our starting note, C, played an octave higher. The notes of the chromatic scale are as follows: C, C#/Db, D, D#/Eb, E, F, F#/Gb, G, G#/Ab, A, A#/Bb, B, C. In essence, the chromatic scale includes all twelve of the notes used in Western music.

Your guitar's fingerboard is a great example of the chromatic scale and its half-step pattern. If we start at the E note of the chromatic scale, and reference this to our low-E string in the fretboard diagram below, we can see that our chromatic scale lines up with the first 12 frets on the guitar.

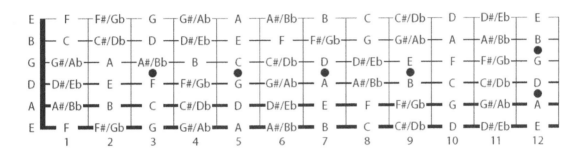

Understanding Scale Diagrams

For our purposes, we'll be focusing on two types of scales, the *pentatonic minor* and the *major* scales. These two scales, and most scales in western music, are built by selecting a starting note and using scale-specific whole-step and half-step patterns.

Rather than write out every individual fret numbers and string positions of each note in every scale, scales are often written out by using small grids populated with dots and numbers. These diagrams are structured and oriented in the same way as chord boxes. Vertical lines represent fret divisions and horizontal lines represent the different guitar strings. In effect, they serve the same purpose for learning scales that chord diagrams do for learning chords. They increase readability. Let's take a look at the *A minor pentatonic scale* diagram, and tablature, for example.

A Minor Pentatonic

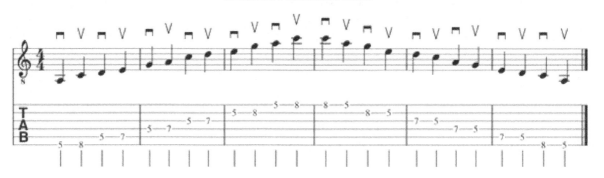

Scale Study:

A Minor Pentatonic Scale

In this diagram we can immediately identify a few pieces of crucial information. We have a fret indicator on the bottom left of our diagram which tells us what part of the fingerboard to play this pattern on. This fret number is often placed on the fret before the scale position to increase clarity for the diagram itself.

Next, we have an array of two differently colored dots that tell us which notes produce the scale on the guitar. Our red-filled dots tell us where the root or tonic notes are fretted in our scale. The black dots tell us where our following scale degrees, or notes, are positioned within a given scale. Finally, we have finger numbers placed on each note (dot) to give us the most ergonomic method for playing each scale. These numbers correspond with the fingers on your fretting hand.

1: Index / Pointer Finger
2: Middle Finger
3: Ring Finger
4: Pinkie Finger

Side Note: In your study or personal research while learning the guitar, you may come across some scale patterns that *don't* list finger positions. If you come across patterns without finger numbers, play the scale in the way that does not compromise proper fret-hand technique. Always keep your fret-hand's wrist as straight as possible to avoid injury.

Pentatonic Minor Scales

Now that we have a better understanding of what scale charts do for us as guitarists, let's take a closer look at the genres that use the pentatonic minor scale, when *we* can use it, and how to use the pattern in different areas on the fingerboard.

The minor pentatonic scale is commonly used in genres like blues, jazz, and rock. Many different artists use the pentatonic scale because of its unique sound and its ergonomic pattern across the fingerboard.

Here's a list of songs that use the A minor pentatonic scale:
"Stairway to Heaven" – Led Zeppelin
"Dani California" – Red Hot Chili Peppers
"While My Guitar Gently Weeps" – The Beatles

The term, *Pentatonic*, can be broken down into two parts: *Penta* = Five, *Tonic* = Note. Therefore, a pentatonic scale is a five-note scale.

In our explanation of scales at the beginning of this section, we talked a little bit about how scales are made with patterns. We said that each scale, regardless of the scale in question, is built with a series of whole steps and half steps or a combination of the two. The A minor pentatonic scale also follows this concept of patterns when discussing how to play the scale on the fingerboard.

The minor pentatonic scale pattern is as follows: (W+H), W, W, (W+H), W.
Looks confusing, right? At this point, I'd agree. I'm sure you didn't expect math to be involved when you picked up this guide. That said, let's break this "code" down into usable parts so we can build a minor pentatonic scale from the ground up.

When we refer to our pentatonic scale as an *A* minor pentatonic scale, we know that our root note is going to be an A note. This happens to be our first note on our scale diagram.

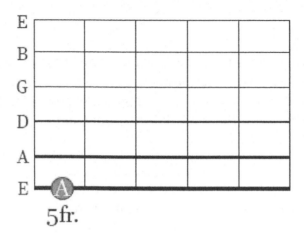

So, right now we know that our first note, the root, is an A. We can also find this root note on the 5th fret of the sixth string by using our notes of the fingerboard diagram.

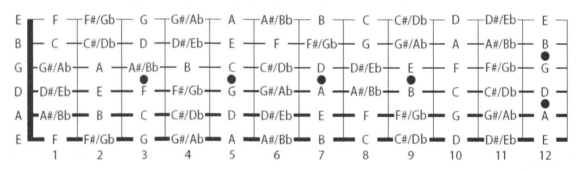

Now we need to transition from our first note, A, to the second note by combining a whole-step with a half step. From our discussion of whole steps and half steps, we know that a whole-step is equal to two frets and a half step is equal to one fret. If we take this whole step, starting from the 5th fret of the sixth string, we'd land on the 7th fret of the sixth string. But, according to our pattern, we still need to add one more half step. If we add one more fret to our 7th-fret position, we'll land on the 8th fret, which is a C note.

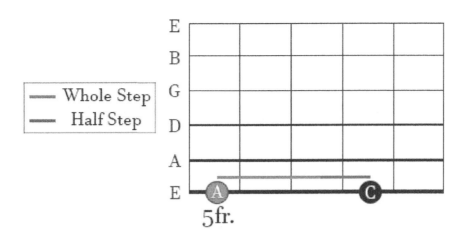

Unfortunately not a C-note in the monetary sense (hundred dollar bill, y'all!), but we now have the second note of the A minor pentatonic scale, C.

Next, by looking at our pattern, we can see that we need to move up one whole-step (W) for the third note of our scale.

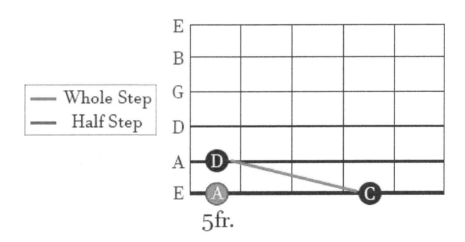

With one whole-step up from our last note C, we arrive at the third note of this pentatonic scale, D. Three down, two to go.

Next, we need to move from our D note to the fourth note of the scale, E. We can consult our minor pentatonic pattern, or formula if you like, and see that we'll be moving up by one whole-step, or two frets. Doing so moves us from D to E, the fourth note of the minor pentatonic scale.

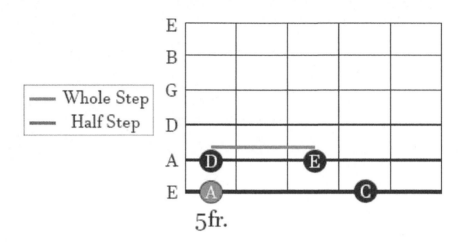

Lastly, we'll move up by the equivalent value of three frets, or one whole-step and one half-step, to the fifth note of the A minor pentatonic scale, G.

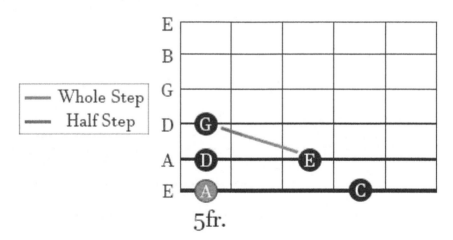

At this point, we've taken our minor pentatonic pattern and used it with the A note as our tonic to build a simple, five-note scale. The notes of this scale are A, C, D, E, G, and as long as we use the minor pentatonic pattern provided at the beginning, we can create an A minor pentatonic scale throughout the fingerboard. But this scale seems somewhat incomplete doesn't it?

118

The reason for this disparity between our original minor pentatonic diagram and the one we've just created can be traced back to two concepts, *pitch class* and *octaves*.

On Pitch Class and Octaves

When we play a scale, such as the pentatonic, we normally use a specified number of notes given by the type of scale we're playing. In pentatonic scales, we know that the specified number of notes is five because of our knowledge of the prefix "penta" in pentatonic. Major and minor *diatonic* scales follow a similar pattern with seven note-scales but we'll get to that shortly.

The interesting things about scales, and music in general, is that the pitches we use will repeat in different pitch classes. This means that all of the notes in our chromatic scale (C-C#/Db-D-D#/Eb-E-F-F#/Gb-G-G#/Ab-A-A#/Bb-B-C) will have higher- or lower-pitched versions of the same note when played on the guitar. This is also referred to as different octaves, or ranges of the guitar.

To see this in action, play the root note of the A minor pentatonic scale, A on the 5th fret of the low-E string, and the 7th fret on the D-string at the same time. Do the notes sound similar? The reason they sound similar is because you've just played two A notes, i.e., an *octave*. This concept is made clearer by looking at the red-filled notes detailed in our A minor pentatonic scale diagram.

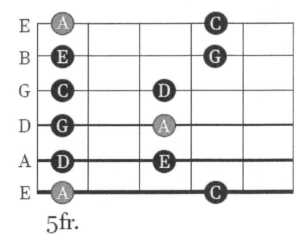

5fr.

Notice how all of the A notes are highlighted in red within the minor pentatonic scale. These notes, while similar, are actually the same notes repeated in different pitch classes. It is because of the concept of pitch classes that we're able to complete the previously half-constructed scale to the scale diagram's ten-note expression. Once we end the series of our first five notes in this scale, we can repeat the pattern, starting on the 7th fret of the D-string, ending up with another series of A, C, D, E, and G notes.

119

Minor Pentatonic Scale: In Summary

As a last point on the minor pentatonic scale, I'd like to discuss the idea of moving these patterns around the fingerboard to achieve different scales based on where the scale is played. In our example with the A minor pentatonic, we used the 5th fret on the sixth string to build and complete our scale. But what if we wanted to play a G minor pentatonic scale or a B minor pentatonic scale?

Remember when we first started discussing barre chords and their root notes? Scale patterns work rather similarly to these barre chord shapes. Both barre chords and scales feature tonic notes that describe how the chord or scale will be constructed. When playing scales, we can use this root note system to change our scale by simply moving the described pattern up or down the fretboard.

If we wanted to play a G minor pentatonic, we'd simply need to find the G note on our notes of the fretboard diagram and position the pattern accordingly. In this case, we'd find the 3rd fret of the sixth string to find our root note, G, and play the scale like we did in our A minor pentatonic example. Take a look at the diagram below to see how the pattern remains the same while the notes of our scale change when we reposition our pattern.

G Minor Pentatonic Scale

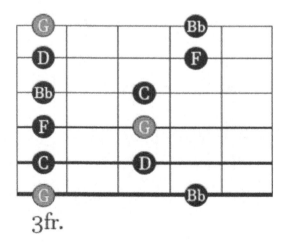

3fr.

Finding the B minor pentatonic scale is no different. We'd look for the B root on our sixth string, find it on the 7th fret, and again, play the pattern accordingly. If we move our pattern up to the 7th fret, our notes change again.

B Minor Pentatonic Scale

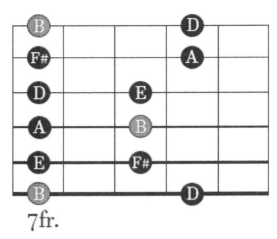

7fr.

By memorizing the pentatonic scale pattern, we can quickly adjust our scale position to suit the key signature of a song.

Major Scales

The major scale is a seven-note scale pattern used frequently, arguably the most common scale, in many different genres of music such as pop, country, rock, jazz, and, in certain cases, blues.

The major scale, like the minor pentatonic scale is derived from the chromatic scale using the following half-step (H) / whole-step (W) pattern: W, W, H, W, W, W, H. This pattern is worth memorizing!

Let's begin building our scale from the tonic note, C.

When we add our major scale pattern to this tonic, complete with whole steps and half steps, we end up with the following notes: C, D, E, F, G, A, B, C. How did we do that?

Let's write the notes out to see how adding half steps and whole steps will build our major scale.

Starting Note = C
C + One Whole-Step = D
D + One Whole-Step = E
E + One Half-Step = F
F + One Whole-Step = G

G + One Whole-Step = A
A + One Whole Step = B
B + One Half-Step = C (Octave)

In our whole-step additions, we skip the accidental notes (sharps and flats) and arrive at the next note in our major scale.

When we repeat this pattern on the fingerboard, we're left with something that looks like this diagram:

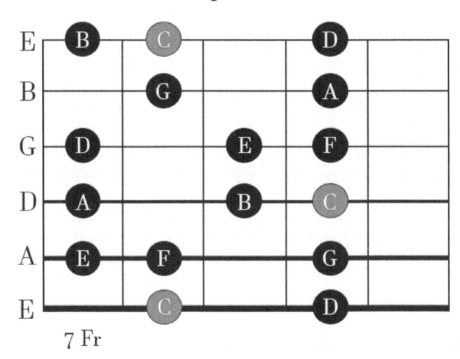

In this case, we started on the 8th fret of the low E-string (C-note) and added our notes according to the major scale pattern (W, W, H, W, W, W, H) where we eventually ended up with our C major scale.

Just like the minor pentatonic scale, the major scale patterns can be moved around the fingerboard to suit certain parts of songs. To demonstrate the effect of pattern movement on scale definition, let's move this pattern down three frets and see how it impacts our scale.

A Major Scale

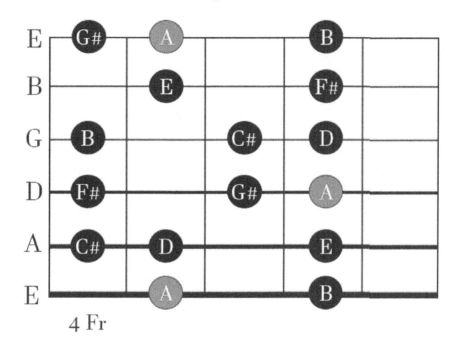

4 Fr

Notice how the pattern remains exactly the same as in our C major example. Both scales follow the same shape but our scale has effectively changed from a C major scale to an A major scale because of where we've moved the scale on the fingerboard. Similar to our discussion of scale pattern movement with the A minor pentatonic scale pattern, this has to do with our red-finger positions or root notes of each scale.

Regardless of where we place this pattern on the fingerboard, the scale will remain major because the original whole-step and half-step pattern remains the same.

Now let's talk about how these notes are ordered based on their half- and whole-step formations.

Scale Degrees – How are Notes Ordered?

In any *heptatonic* (seven-note) scale, like our major scale, each of the seven notes has a name that refers to its numerical position within the scale. These position descriptions are called *scale degrees*. In heptatonic scales like the major scale, scale degrees conveniently use the numbers one through seven to describe the degrees, though the first scale degree is commonly referred to as the *tonic* or *root* note. They are as follows:

First – *Root / Tonic*
Second – *Supertonic*
Third – *Mediant*
Fourth – *Subdominant*
Fifth – *Dominant*
Sixth – *Submediant*
Seventh – *Subtonic* (Natural Minor Scale) / *Leading Tone* (Major Scale)
Eighth – *Tonic (Octave)*

Once a particular tonic is chosen, the scale degrees help us identify the particular note sequence within a scale.

Using the note C as the tonic of our major scale, we can compare this scale to our scale degrees listed above:

First – *Root / Tonic* – C
Second – *Supertonic* – D
Third – *Mediant* – E
Fourth – *Subdominant* – F
Fifth – *Dominant* – G
Sixth – *Submediant* – A
Seventh – *Leading Tone* – B
Eighth – *Octave* – C

Understanding these terms, whether you use the note numbers or the name of the scale degree, is useful in that each scale degree will always be the same regardless of which seven-note scale is used. For instance, in the C major scale example above, we know that the *dominant* or 5th scale degree is a G note. If we replace the C major scale with an A major scale in our example, the notes change but the scale degrees remain the same.

First – *Root / Tonic* – A
Second – *Supertonic* – B
Third – *Mediant* – C#
Fourth – *Subdominant* – D
<u>Fifth – *Dominant* – E</u>
Sixth – *Submediant* – F#
Seventh – *Leading Tone* – G#
Eighth – *Octave* – A

124

We could put any major scale in place with this formula and the degrees would never change. We could substitute A major for Bb major, F major for G major, the fact remains that scale degrees are set in stone when used with major scales.

Notes and the Spaces Between: Intervals

Intervals

C Major Scale

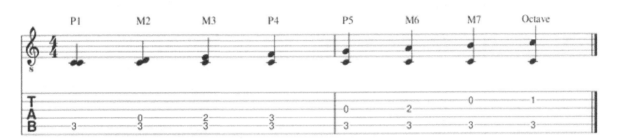

Now that we have a better understanding of how scales work, it's important to take a closer look at the relationship between the notes on the fingerboard. The most basic relationship between these notes is called an *interval*.

In the beginning of this guide, we defined an interval as the distance between two notes. A to C is an interval, B to F# is an interval, as long as two notes are compared, an interval exists between them.

That said, there are specific names for the main intervals that coincide with a set number of semitones or half steps.

Before we dive into how we can determine an interval between two notes on our own, let's take a look at some of the most common intervals in the grid below. Each interval in this list is first expressed by the name of the interval, followed by the interval's abbreviation, and ends with the number of semitones or half steps that make up the interval. We've also placed a few different tunes on the right side of the table to help give you a better idea of what these intervals sound like in songs.

***Note: The perfect unison interval is the "interval" between one note played twice or two instruments playing the same note simultaneously.*

Interval Name	Abbreviation	Semitones	Song
Perfect Unison	P1	0	
Minor Second	m2	1	Theme from *Jaws*
Major Second	M2	2	"Happy Birthday"
Minor Third	m3	3	"Seven Nation Army" (The White Stripes)
Major Third	M3	4	"Ob-La-Di Ob-La Da" (Beatles)
Perfect Fourth	P4	5	"Amazing Grace"
Diminished Fifth	d5	6	Theme from *The Simpsons*
Augmented Fourth	A4	6	Theme from *The Simpsons*
Perfect Fifth	P5	7	Theme from *Star Wars*
Minor Sixth	m6	8	"In My Life" (Beatles)
Major Sixth	M6	9	"Jingle Bells"
Minor Seventh	m7	10	Theme from *Star Trek*
Major Seventh	M7	11	"Take on Me" (A-Ha)
Perfect Octave	P8	12	"Sweet Child O' Mine" (Guns N' Roses)

Intervals can be kind of confusing so let's break this beast of a table down into digestible chunks.

The first thing we have to discuss is how an interval's name expresses the number of semitones within the interval.

The Number Side of Intervals

To start, each interval has two parts - The number (Major ***Third***, Perfect ***Fifth***, Minor ***Second***) and the quality or type of interval (***Major*** Third, ***Perfect*** Fifth, ***Minor*** Second).

The number portion of an interval is the easiest part to figure out. To do so, we first take two different notes and decide which interval has the lower pitch. Let's determine which interval lies between C and A. For simplicity's sake, we'll say that C has the lower pitch of the two notes.

Now we need to return to our discussion of major scales and the notes that major scales contain. Since C has the lowest pitch of our two notes, we'll go ahead and use the notes or scale degrees within the C major scale to determine our interval.

The C major scale consists of the following notes or scale degrees: C(1), D(2), E(3), F(4), G(5), A(6), B(7), C(8). Now we need to count the notes (including the starting and ending notes) to figure out the number portion of our interval. Starting on the note C the count would look like this: C1 - D2 - E3 - F4 - G5 - **A6**

Great! We figured out how to determine where the number side of intervals come from. By counting the notes ranging from C through A, we know that our interval will be a sixth of some type. Now we need to figure out how to determine the quality or type of an interval.

Interval Qualities

Each interval in the list of common intervals above has a "type" or "quality" given before the number portion of the interval. These qualities include perfect, augmented, diminished, major, and minor.

The unison, fourth, fifth, and octave are the only intervals that can be *perfect*. Perfect intervals are often said to be "perfect" because of how resolute and pleasant they sound. That said, perfect intervals can be raised by a semitone to produce an augmented interval or lowered by a semitone to produce a diminished interval.

For example, if we took a perfect fifth (seven semitones or half steps) and lowered the interval by one semitone, we would have six semitones in our interval, producing a *diminished* fifth. Conversely, if we raised the interval by one semitone to eight semitones, we'd have an *augmented* fifth.

Major intervals behave similarly. The second, third, sixth and seventh are the only intervals that can be *major*. Major intervals can be raised by a semitone to produce an augmented interval or lowered to produce a minor interval.

For instance, if we decreased the number of semitones in a major third (four semitones) by one semitone, we'd be left with three semitones or a *minor* third. On the other hand, if we increased the number of semitones in the major third interval by one semitone, we'd have five semitones or an *augmented* third.

Determining the Quality of an Interval

Let's continue our C to A interval example from above.

Because major scales are built using the following set of intervals, Root Note (Perfect Unison) - Major 2nd - Major 3rd - Perfect 4th - Perfect 5th - Major 6th - Major 7th - Perfect Octave, we can quickly determine what "type" of interval we're dealing with by comparing the number portion of the interval to the scale degree position in the major scale.

When we counted our interval in the last step of our interval example, we went from C to A which gave us a sixth. If we look at the C major scale, we can also see that the note A is in our scale and falls on the sixth scale degree.

Because the note is in the scale, we can use the interval listed in the staff above to find the quality of the interval. Since the sixth scale degree is a major interval and the note A is in our C major scale, our example is complete. The interval between C and A is a major sixth.

Now let's say that our happy little example wasn't this convenient and the interval in question included the notes C and A#. What would we do then?

The steps to determine the interval, except the last step, don't really change in this case. We'd still count the notes from C to A, and we'd still reference the C major scale to verify that the second note of the interval is in fact in the scale. The only thing we'd need to do now is figure out how the higher-pitched note of the interval differs from what note (A) should line up in the major scale. In other words, the number will remain the same, a 6th in this case.

From the section of the C major scale, we know that the note A falls into the C major scale but A# does not. We also know that A# is one half-step or one semitone higher than A. If we reference the interval quality section above, we'd know that this difference produces an augmented sixth because the note A, the second part of our major sixth interval, was raised by one half-step. We would call this interval an *Augmented Sixth*, or A6 (aug6).

And for intervals that start with C major, this method is excellent. But, what if the interval didn't start on the root note C?

What if we wanted to determine what the interval is between the notes F# and B or B and D? Based on our previous example we'd have to know or look up the notes of the F# or B major scale, respectively. depending on which note has the lower pitch, and use the scale to figure out the interval. For beginners, unless you're on a Mozart-level of "beginner", you probably don't know every note in every major scale.

Fortunately, there is another way we can count intervals. Rather than using the method above, we can count the semitones or half-steps between two notes using the chromatic scale. Let's try this method with the notes D and G.

In this case, we'll say that D is the note with the lower pitch of the two notes within this interval. Now we need to count through the *spaces between notes* of the chromatic scale to determine how many half-steps it takes to get from D to G.

This method of counting means that the starting point of our count begins on the first "space" between notes after the root of our interval. Rather than counting the root note first, "C(1), C# / Db(2), D(3)", we'd count the space after the root note like this: "C, **Space**(1), C# / Db, **Space**(2), D. In the interval between C and D, we have two spaces or semitones, giving us a major second.

The Chromatic Scale:

D - (D# / Eb) - E - F - (F# / Gb) - G - (G# / Ab) - A - (A# / Bb) - B - C - (C# / Db) - D

Counting through the chromatic scale from C to A would look like this:

D **(1)** D# / Eb **(2)** E **(3)** F **(4)** F# / Gb **(5)** G

Based on the counting here, we can see that the note G is five semitones away from the note D. Looking at the table of the common intervals, we can see that an interval of five semitones is a perfect fourth.

Interval Name	Abbreviation	Semitones	Song
Perfect Fourth	P4	5	"Amazing Grace"

Other intervals can be counted in the same way. For instance, the interval between F and G consists of two semitones, producing a major second interval.

F **(1)** F# / Gb **(2)** G

If it isn't already clear, intervals are the musical building blocks that support concepts like chords, scales, and melodies. Intervals allow us to measure the distances between notes in the songs we learn, the riffs we write, and give us the ability to speak in a musical "shorthand" that other musicians recognize. It'd be kind of hard to tell a saxophone player to play the notes of the third fret of the low E and A string, right?

Recognizing intervals also helps us explain why some guitar parts in songs feel better to us than others. As we mentioned in the earlier sections of this guide, minor chords tend to have a sadder sound. This is a direct result of the use of a minor third in the chord, which has a less "happy sound" than say a major third or perfect fifth.

Although some of this information can be dense and theoretical, by "hitting the books" with the theory behind scales and chords, you'll be able to better understand why a song makes you feel a certain way. In turn, you'll be better set to recognize what gives a song a certain feeling by using the intervals responsible in your own writing and playing.

Getting Started with Melodies

From what we've learned thus far, we have the basic bones of a song. We've learned the essential chords that make up the pop, rock, and country songs you know and love. We've also learned how two scale patterns work and how scale patterns can be moved around the fingerboard to produce different scales. That said, we're still missing something. That something turns out to be what is referred to in music-speak as a "melody."

A melody is a standalone tune that people tend to remember from a song long after it's played.

So, how are melodies different from chords? The answer is that while both chords and melodies have notes *within* them, a melody is a series of notes sung or played individually, where a chord is a group of notes played at the same time.

As you study guitar, you will come to find that the two definitions do mingle at times, but for our purposes, note that a melody typically features several single-note phrases while chords feature multiple notes played at the same time.

The Notes of the Fingerboard

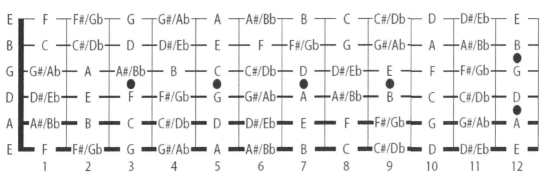

As you practice the guitar, you'll start to notice patterns in the note names that emerge across the fingerboard. As a simple example, take a look at the low- and high-E strings. Notice how the note names are exactly the same on each fret position. To help you in this process, we've laid out all of the notes spanning the first 12 frets of the fingerboard. These notes repeat after the 12th fret and continue until the end of the fingerboard. This knowledge will open doors across the fingerboard and allows you to play any chord in any position, provided you know the shape and the root of the chord.

What is Alternate Picking?

As you study the guitar, you'll eventually find that guitarists' technique varies widely across genres. There're strummers, pluckers, pickers, and even those who combine these elements in hybrid picking. One technique that is an absolute must in terms of building speed and capability in your picking hand is *alternate picking*.

Alternate picking occurs when you take a pick in your picking hand and instead of using *only* downstrokes or upstrokes, you combine the two and alternate between upstrokes and downstrokes.

The benefit of alternate picking as opposed to solely using downstrokes is the speed that comes with the technique. By alternating up and down strokes, you no longer need to bring your pick back to its original position above or below the strings. This in turn, allows for a more efficient play style. In addition to speed, your melody lines and solos will see vast improvement in rhythm and clarity when using alternate picking.

A terrific example of alternate picking is Dick Dale's surf rock anthem, "Miserlou".

Let's take a look at a few exercises and see if we can't alternate pick ourselves. First up is a simple alternate picking pattern that incorporates both open and fretted strings. This exercise alternates between upstrokes and downstrokes throughout the exercise so be sure to grab your metronome and keep your eye on the up and down bow symbols along the staff!

Alternate Picking Exercise 1

In the next exercise, we'll start adding in a few extra notes on each string. This exercise follows a similar upstroke and downstroke pattern, but it should feel slightly more complicated with the added 4th-fret notes. After getting comfortable with it, try setting your metronome a bit faster for this exercise. Around 90bpm should do it, but if you feel you can do it faster, please go ahead and do so!

Alternate Picking Exercise 2

Your First Melody

Congratulations! Now that we have a sound knowledge of beginner chord structures and rhythm patterns, it's time to start on our first single-string melody. This is a traditional melody and features alternate picking throughout. If the alternate picking gives you trouble, feel free to play this melody in the way that feels comfortable for you.

First Melody

Twinkle, Twinkle, Little Star

Jane Taylor ~ 1806

More Melodies

Next up is the classical music classic, "Ode to Joy" by Ludwig van Beethoven. Was Ludwig a guitar player? Absolutely not. But, the melody is a perfect example of how a simple key or scale like C major can sound great, if not timeless. If you look closely at this piece, you'll notice that it uses all of the notes in our C major scale pattern. Here's the C major scale diagram again, for reference.

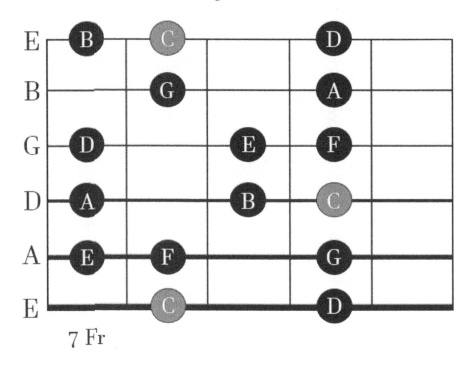

136

Symphony No. 9 Op. 125

Ode to Joy

Ludwig van Beethoven ~ 1824

Up next is the quintessential birthday song, "Happy Birthday"! This song is arranged in the key of A major, meaning that we can see all of the notes played in this melody in our A major scale. Here's the A major scale diagram again for your review.

A Major Scale

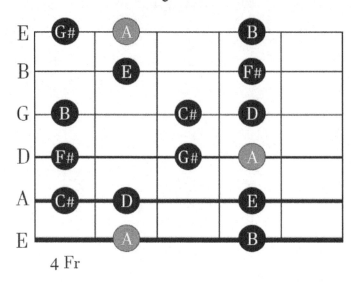

Happy Birthday

A holiday classic, "Jingle Bells" lays the groundwork for rhythm study on the guitar. This version is a single-string arrangement and is another great opportunity to practice your alternate picking.

Jingle Bells

James Lord Pierpont

Guitar Techniques Using the Minor Pentatonic Scale

If you've ever listened to any guitar solo, or really any song with guitar, you've likely noticed that guitarists seldom drone on and on with the same technique. It's more common that guitar players will utilize the expressive options within a variety of techniques. While all songs in Western music revolve around a series of generally acknowledged scales, the emotion of music stems from dynamic playing within the context of each song.

As we discuss these guitar techniques, we'll be implementing the techniques with a scale we've already covered, the minor pentatonic scale, to cement the pattern deep within our guitar knowledge. This whole section revolves around fun and exciting bends and slides with the minor pentatonic scale. The minor pentatonic scale is a staple in popular rock soloing and is one of the most versatile scales that one can play on the guitar.

Slides

An absolutely essential guitar technique, the *slide*, is defined by fretting a note on any given string, or strings, plucking said string, and sliding the fretted note up or down any given number of frets. Whether you only go up or down one fret, whether you scale the entire fingerboard with this technique, whether you use your pinkie, ring, middle, or index finger, as long as you slide any finger from one note to another, it's still considered a slide. Make sure that you really dig in and drag your finger along the fretboard when playing these slide exercises below.

Scale Study:

A Minor Pentatonic Scale - Slides

While slides are certainly used with variations of single-note transitions, it's often a useful technique to implement slides into your chord playing. Sliding chords are often used in many different genres like jazz, blues, rock, and sometimes pop music.

Let's take a look at a slide using the following dominant seventh chords.

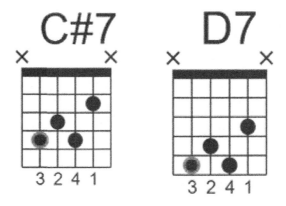

Chord Slides

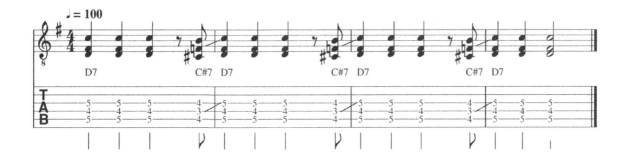

As you play through this tab, you might notice that the $C\#^7$ chord slides right into the D7 chord around the end of measure one and the beginning of measure two. This means that we change from the D^7 to the $C\#^7$ for half a beat at the end of each measure and slide, with all three fingers, back into the D^7 chord at the beginning of the next measure.

Guthrie Govan's "Waves" is an exceptional example of slide technique, though this song is definitely on the higher end of advanced slide technique. It features slides across the fingerboard to achieve interesting note variations as well as an energetic sound.

"Waves" – Guthrie Govan

Additional Slide Examples:
"For the Love of God" – Steve Vai
"Purple Haze" – Jimi Hendrix

Hammer-Ons and Pull-Offs

How to Hammer-On

Hammer-ons, also considered a form of a slur in music, occur when a guitar player takes one played note and immediately replaces it with another note, played on the same string, without plucking the string again. Sounds complicated, right? At first, it certainly seems that way, but it's far easier if we break it down into steps.

1. Fret a note on any string with your index finger
2. Pluck the note with your picking hand
3. Quickly place another finger on the fret above the original note, in other words, "hammering-on" the additional note.

How to Pull-Off

Pulling-off can be looked at as the polar opposite of hammering-on with the guitar; this is also a form of slurring, or legato playing. In this case, we're going to start with our fretting hand on one fret on a single string. Let's use the B-string as an example. Starting with your index finger fretting the second fret of the B-string. Give it a pluck. Once you achieve the clear sound of the resonating string, release, or "pull-off", your index finger from the string. You may notice that the effect this creates is similar to the hammer-on above, but played in reverse.

Below is an example of the A minor pentatonic scale played ascending and descending only using hammer-ons and pull-offs. Take this exercise slow and methodically as this technique takes some time to get used to.

Scale Study

Hammer-ons and Pull-offs using A Pentatonic Minor

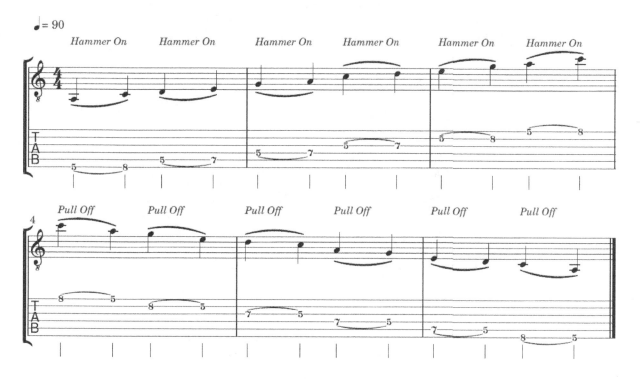

Hammer-On and Pull-Offs Example Songs:

If you're having trouble getting this technique down, take a look at a few of these YouTube videos. These are the quintessential hammer-on and pull-off songs and feature varying levels of difficulty across the board. In addition, using the video speed feature on these clips makes them far easier to digest and understand how exactly to achieve the resulting sounds.

"Thunderstruck" – AC/DC
"Over the Hills and Far Away" – Led Zeppelin
"Wish You Were Here" – Pink Floyd
"The Trooper" – Iron Maiden
"Nervous Breakdown" – Brad Paisley
"Spirit of Radio" – Rush

Bends

Bending, or changing the pitch of any given note by stretching a string, adds a dynamic flavor to music known throughout many genres. Heavy metal, blues and country licks often feature this pitch-increasing technique in several different fashions. Bends range in difficulty from the simple techniques like full bends and half step bends, to the more complex techniques like quarter-step bends, reverse bends, multi-string bends, and oblique bends.

How to Bend

Bending guitar strings requires us to stretch strings, with appropriate pressure, to achieve our desired note. The act of bending and stretching guitar strings involves leverage provided by the use of both your fingers and your wrist. This leverage is easiest to create when we use more than one finger. Ideally, we'd be using three fingers: your ring finger to fret the note, and your middle and index to provide added support. This may feel uncomfortable at first as you're likely to use your index and middle finger most often when starting out. That said, bending with multiple fingers will "share the wealth" of finger pain and reduce the likelihood of fatigue and repetitive motion injuries.

Once you have the desired note and the necessary bend to achieve said note, it's time to start plucking strings. With all three fingers at the ready, pluck your original fretted note. After the note rings clear, go ahead and push upward or pull downward on the string and listen to the new note. If done correctly, the sound should have increased in pitch.

As you start to stretch, push, pull on your strings, it's also important to note that some string gauges are better suited to bends than others. This isn't to say that a particular brand of strings will be easier or harder, just that thicker strings will be harder to stretch.

Full-Step (or Whole-Step) Bends

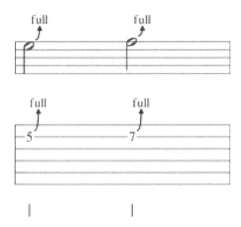

Full-Step Bend = Original Note + Two Frets (like a whole step!)

As we mentioned above, bending a note on the guitar is essentially pushing up a fretted note to lengthen the string and subsequently increase the pitch of said note. In guitar-speak, when we perform a "full bend", what we are actually doing is increasing the fretted note, whichever it may be, by one whole step, or two half steps.

If we say to bend the 5th fret on the second string, an E-note in standard tuning, by one full step, we mean to say that we're bending (increasing) this note to an F#. The same can be said for any note on the fingerboard.

Half-Step Bends

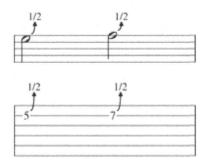

Half-step bends are similar to full-step bends with the only difference being the amount we lengthen the string in our bend. A full-step bend is adding two semitone values (two frets) to our original note. A half-step bend adds one semitone value to our original note.

Let's refer back to our original example from the previous section. We have our original note, "E" played on the 5th fret on the second string. If we were to raise this E-note one half step on the keyboard, we'd get an F-note, or the note produced by fretting the 6th fret on the second string.

As we're learning how to perform half-step bends or full-step bends, it may be beneficial to play the target note of the bend *before* we start bending strings. In the case of our half step bend, our goal note will be on the 6th fret of the fifth (B) string.

When we precede our bends with our goal note, we achieve a better understanding of how much finger pressure is needed to bend the string and we avoid going too sharp or too flat in each bend we perform. Once you have a good idea of the pressure required to achieve half- and full-step bends, playing the target note before we bend isn't necessary. Use this practice to learn the amount of finger pressure needed to bend a half- or whole-step above the note until the amount of finger pressure becomes natural to you.

Songs that Use Bends Effectively
Both Stevie Ray Vaughan and David Gilmour use bending in impressive ways in these two tunes. Check them out to get a better idea of what bending can sound like in two totally different styles!
"Little Wing" – Stevie Ray Vaughan
"Shine on You Crazy Diamond" – Pink Floyd

Let's try and give the bend a shot. Remember that a whole-step bend requires us to add enough string tension to raise the pitch of the note two frets higher than our starting note. A half-step bend requires enough string tension to raise the pitch of our note one-fret higher than our starting note. Note that there is no tempo provided in this exercise. You should perform this exercise at a speed that is comfortable for you, making sure that each note is played clearly. *Keep an eye on which notes are full-bends and which are half-bends.*

Scale Study:

A Minor Pentatonic Bends

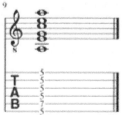

Vibrato

Vibrato is similar to bending because it involves taking a single note and adding tension to the original note. Where vibrato differs from bending is in the relief of string tension and the repetitious nature of the technique. Vibrato combines bending with a sort of "shake" produced by the arm and wrist of your fretting hand.

Recognizing Vibrato in Tab and Sheet Music

The symbol for vibrato is easily recognized because of its unique wave-like form. The vibrato symbol features an oscillating black line that resembles a sawtooth pattern.

Here's a figure of the vibrato line:

And a figure of the vibrato line above a tabbed note:

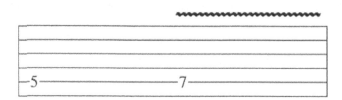

There may be times where you come across a vibrato line with shorter or longer intervals between waves. Shorter intervals dictate shorter, more rapid string vibration, where longer intervals express longer and more deliberate string vibrations.

Vibrato – Hand Positioning

To perform this technique, we'll need to grab the guitar and take a look at our fretting hand. Though the rule states that your thumb should support your left hand by taking a position on the back-middle section of the neck, vibrato tends to be somewhat difficult with this position. To allow for easier leverage, we want to place our thumb toward the top of the neck, leaving our palm space between our thumb and index finger fairly open. Vibrato, like bending, is made easiest when we share the string tension between several fingers. The three most common fingers are again, the index, middle, and ring fingers.

Once you've identified the note to which you'll add the vibrato effect, go ahead and line your ring finger on the note with your other two fingers following. Pluck the note and start the vibrato technique by slowly pushing and pulling on the chosen string. Though it may seem counterintuitive, the fluctuation of the original note does not come from pressure created by your finger joints. You can certainly do this, but there is a better way.

The best way to achieve consistent variation across your vibrato is by employing your wrist and elbow in this technique. This allows for even pressure and more strength due to the larger muscle groups that support these joints.

It is important to remember that, while good vibrato can accentuate your notes and color your melodies and solos, this technique can be a challenge for most novice guitar players. It's critical to avoid discouragement and understand that each technique is a form of expression in music and will come with time and practice.

By starting slow, you can start to hear the variations of said note, similar to how reverb works in a hallway. The effect we're after is the central beginning note with added variations to create a fluctuation of said note.

The A Minor Pentatonic with Vibrato
Ascending

<u>Vibrato Essentials – Songs to Review</u>

Both of these guitar phenoms use vibrato throughout these songs, yet, the result is different in each case. B.B. King tends to add and release tension in his vibrato in smaller ranges and faster variations. In contrast, Angus Young, in the beginning of his "Back in Black" solo, uses vibrato in wide, lengthy ranges and tends to repeatedly stretch the notes much slower than B.B. King.

"The Thrill is Gone" – B.B. King

"Back in Black" – AC/DC

Double Stops

Double stops are the proverbial "middle child" between the lines of single notes that create melodies and the multiple notes played together in chords. Double stopping is a technique where a musician plays two notes together at the same time instead of one or three notes. This technique adds color and expression to your playing and features prominent use in genres like blues or country.

You will notice below that we have a similar concept to that of power chords. We aren't playing single notes, we aren't playing chords, we are simply playing intervals.

Take a look at this exercise to see how double stops are played.

Scale Study:

A Minor Pentatonic with Double Stops

Exercises with the A Minor Pentatonic Scale

Scale work is an absolute must in any guitarist's daily practice session. Studying pattern variations in scale work will help you develop your own unique style and play with confidence when confronting unique melody lines or song sections. The exercises placed here should be played near the beginning of your daily practice sessions and take between five and ten minutes to complete.

A Minor Pentatonic
Exercise One

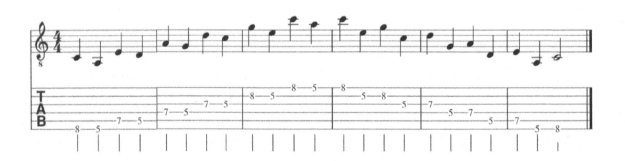

A Minor Pentatonic
Exercise Two

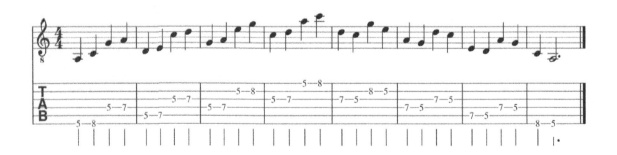

152

A Minor Pentatonic

Exercise Three

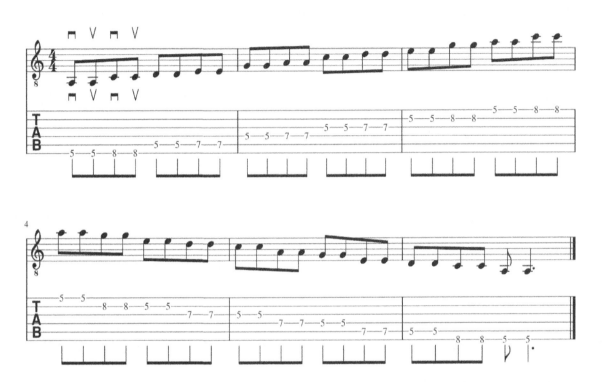

Making a Solo: Combining the Soloing Techniques

Now that we've studied our scales and learned essential soloing techniques, it's time we combine these techniques into a solo of our own. This next exercise uses all of the concepts we just covered and is an example of how you might write your own solos when you feel ready.

A Bluesy Solo

A Minor Pentatonic Scale

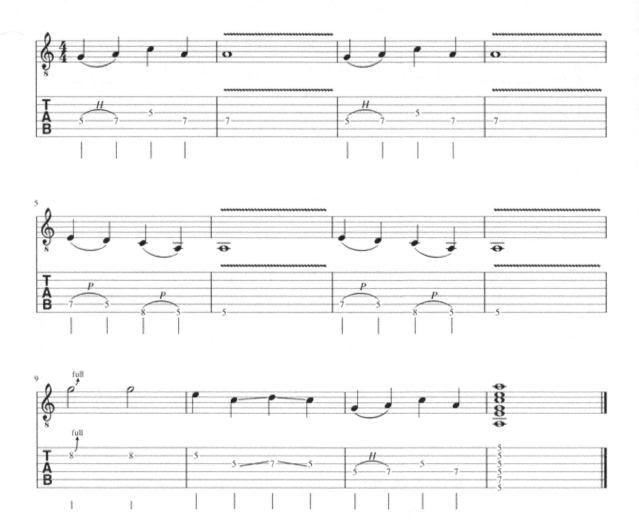

The Blues

Arguably one of the most foundational genres of guitar-centric music today, the blues genre is home to many celebrated guitar greats. Some guitarists who are archetypes of the blues style are Albert King, Stevie Ray Vaughan, Eric Clapton, Jimi Hendrix, Bonnie Raitt, Derek Trucks, Susan Tedeschi; the list goes on. This section will break down the basics of the blues to help you gain an understanding of what the "secret sauce" of blues is, how to break it down, and how to implement blues knowledge into your playing. Let's get started!

The 12-Bar Blues

The 12-bar blues is an extremely common arrangement when discussing blues, and proves useful in discussing music with other musicians. It's important to note that this song form is not exclusive to guitar. As you progress in your playing and start talking and playing with other musicians, you'll find that blues saxophonists, bassists, pianists, and drummers all understand the 12-bar blues as an essential song form.

Without any further ado, let's take a look at this framework we've heard so much about.

The Bar in 12-Bar Blues

The *bar* in 12-bar refers to the measures between vertical bar lines throughout a given song. These bar lines separate our standard sheet music and tablature into measures. In the 12-bar blues, there are, you guessed it, 12 bars of equal length dispersed throughout an arrangement. The 12-bar blues is almost always played with a 4/4-time signature with each measure featuring four beats in equal value to that of a quarter note.

The 12-Bar Form

We are going to construct a 12-bar blues in the key of A major. Here are our chords in the key of A, with the corresponding major, minor, or diminished roman numerals:

(I) A major, (ii) B minor, (iii) C# minor, (IV) D major, (V) E major, (vi) F# minor, (vii°) G# diminished.

In each 12-bar blues, the song form is split into separate sections for different chords. The first four bars start with the one (I) chord of any given key. In the key of A major (A, B, C#, D, E, F#,

155

G#), the one chord would be A because it is the first note of the scale. If we were playing a 12-bar blues in the key of A major, the A major chord would be played for the first four bars.

In the second set of four bars within this form, another chord is introduced. In a standard 12-bar blues, this chord is often the four (IV) chord of a given key. In our example of A major, this would be the D major chord. The four (IV) chord is played for two bars and then changes back to the original one (I) chord for two more bars.

In the third set of four bars, we have even more changes. First among these changes comes in the ninth bar, switching to the five (V) chord. In our A major example, the V chord turns out to be the E major chord. The V chord is played for four beats and then switches back to the IV chord which is also played for four beats. After this change, we switch back to the I chord for two bars or eight beats.

In blues, this pattern is repeated several times to provide musical support for vocals or to give each musician an opportunity to play a written solo or improvise one on the spot. The 12-bar blues ends when a set number of bars has been completed – often a multiple of 12 – or, in cases of live performance, the musicians agree to bring the song to a close.

Another characteristic of blues music is our dominant seventh chord, which we discussed earlier. Almost all of the chords in blues music are dominant seventh chords.

Let's take play through the 12-bar blues in the key of A major. After you've done this a few times, go ahead and use the A minor pentatonic scale and try to improvise your own solo.

12 Bar Blues in A Major

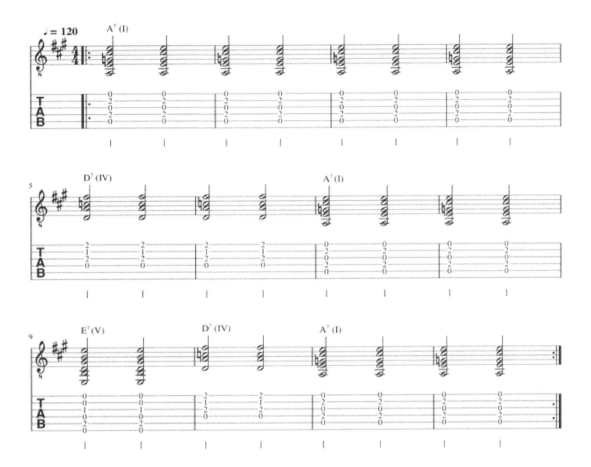

Notice how each row of bars operates differently within this piece. The first set of four bars introduces the one (I) chord and sets the tone for the song. The second set of four bars features a split between the four (IV) chord and one (I) chord, adding a bit of variation. And lastly, the final set of four bars adds a bit of dissonance with the V – IV change and resolves back to the one chord, entailing a feeling of closure.

In Summary:

Well, there you have it. At the start of this guide, you may have been wondering about the specifics about the guitar. How does the guitar work? Could I even play like the greats who established guitar-inclusive or guitar-centric genres? Questions that this guide, hopefully, helped you answer.

We've covered the parts that make up the guitar as well as which guitars are best for each beginner's preferred music stylings. We've learned how to properly hold the guitar to best avoid bad habits and subsequent injuries. We've covered a variety of chords, melodies, and scales to help you turn the songs you love to listen to into the songs you love to play. Overall, this has been, in essence, Guitar 101 – Everything you need to know to get a grasp on learning an instrument with an impressive reputation.

While this guide covers the essential information required to start learning to play this awesome instrument, we can't reiterate enough the importance of playing for enjoyment in your practice. As you improve, it may be tempting to treat the act of playing guitar as a craft to be honed. We start wondering how much faster we could be. How much better can we be? And these are great questions to be asking yourself because improvement and achievement feels great!

That said, placing too much emphasis on "getting good" at the guitar is often cause for needless burnout. If you're stuck on a particular section of a song, or trying to nail some complicated exercise after hours of work with no avail, take a break. Listen to some good tunes and come back to the material later.

As you work to implement these tools and techniques, be sure to explore the songs you enjoy. Whether those songs are at the hearts of guitar-based genres like rock and country, or if you wish to take the guitar to new heights, the guitar, as much as your fingertips may disagree, will always welcome any inspired use.

Finger Dexterity Exercises:

Once you achieve a level of competency with guitar, it's quite normal to question your abilities. Sure, chords come pretty quick once you start tackling the harder shapes, but some fingers, your pinkie in particular, become a sort of dead weight after a certain point. How do we fix this?

A key part of any practice routine should focus on finger dexterity. This often takes place at the beginning of a practice session and can be used as a terrific warmup. Throughout this next section, we'll give you some key exercises with which to hone your craft and make sure your hand-to-hand timing as well as the dexterity of each finger is spot-on.

Single-String Finger Dexterity

The single-string finger dexterity exercise, while it seems simple, is surprisingly useful in learning to play the guitar. When we start playing and really looking for ways to improve our finger dexterity, a common complaint of many guitarists is getting the timing between your picking and fretting hand down. This exercise works to remedy this issue.

In the single-string exercise, we'll want to use the alternate picking technique we learned earlier in this guide. Start by picking the open high-E string, followed by the first four frets with the corresponding fingers of our fretting hand (1st fret: index finger, 2nd fret: middle finger, etc.). If you've done this correctly, you should end the first section of this exercise with your pinkie fretting the 4th fret on the high-E string. We'll repeat this finger positioning pattern in sections from the 5th through the 8th fret and the 9th through the 12th fret. Once we've hit the 12th fret, we'll reverse the pattern and descend back down the frets.

This exercise can be tiresome at first. It's not really musical and probably isn't what you may think of as playing the guitar. That said, using a metronome to analyze your progress and ability is a great way to clarify areas that could be improved. Please take advantage of the metronomes in our resources section if you don't have one. The metronome should be set to 4/4-time at around 100 bpm. If 100 bpm is either too fast or too slow, feel free to adjust the tempo to a comfortable, yet challenging, pace.

Single String Finger Dexterity

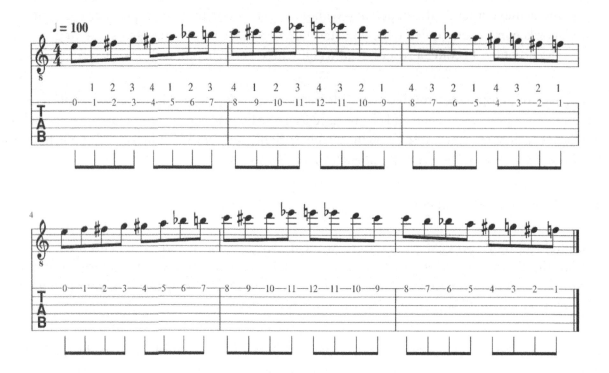

The Spider Exercise

This next exercise uses the fretting hand alone to perform. That's right, give your picking hand a break and focus intently on the individual finger motions of your fretting hand. This exercise runs through several finger combinations, listed by finger number, and again, only uses the fretting hand to complete.

The goal of this exercise is to become comfortable with moving your fingers piecemeal on the fingerboard. That said, this exercise does have one "catch". The catch is that once a set of fingers, whether your index and pinkie or ring and middle, is placed on the fingerboard, they are *not* to be removed until the next set of fingers is placed on the string above or below them.

As an example, take a look at *Spider Variation 1*. Once you've placed your index finger and middle finger on the 5th and 8th fret of the sixth string, you cannot move them until you place your middle

160

and ring fingers on the fifth string. This technique should be followed until each variation of the spider exercise is complete.

Go ahead and take this one slowly and deliberately, and *always* keep two fingers on the fingerboard.

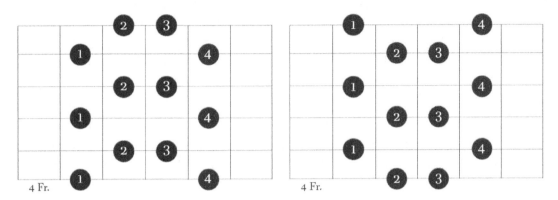

Spider Variation 1

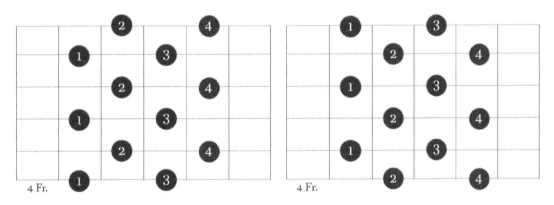

Spider Variation 2

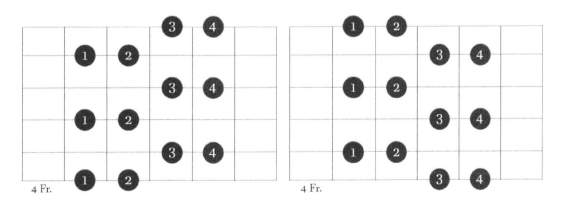

String-Changing Dexterity Exercise

Getting used to quickly moving your fingers is one of the most challenging aspects of learning to play the guitar. The string-changing dexterity exercise, while it's easily the most difficult in this section, provides us with an exceptional opportunity to practice changing strings at a comfortable pace. This exercise uses all four fingers of your fretting hand, making it a useful practice exercise as well as a warm up exercise.

Fret-hand finger positions are listed between the two staffs in each variation of this exercise. As you first practice this exercise, you may find that these finger positions are awkward, unnatural, and uncomfortable. Even so, please follow the finger numbers. The focus of this exercise and each variation is to strengthen all four of the fingers on your fretting hand, and deviating from the positions listed will increase your finger dexterity.

When you're ready, go ahead and set your metronome to 80 bpm or a tempo that feels comfortable for you.

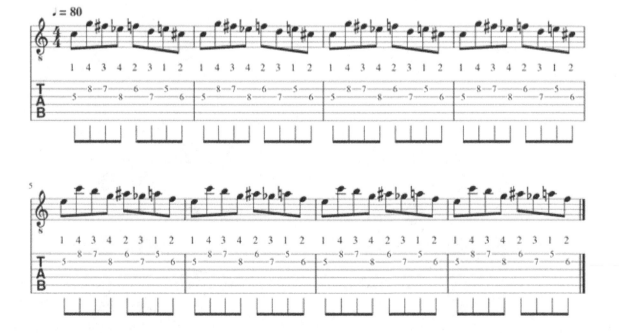

String Change Dexterity
Variation One

String Change Dexterity
Variation Two

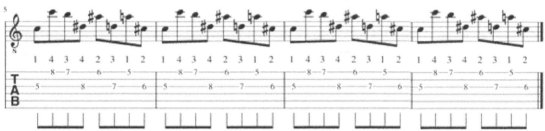

String Change Dexterity
Variation Three

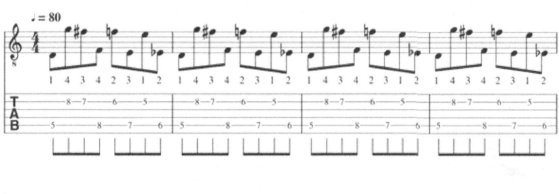

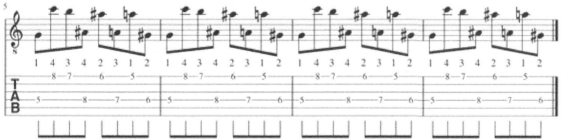

Essential Resources

Tablature

<u>Songsterr</u>
Songsterr is a unique tablature program that allows the community, and professionals, to submit music to thousands of popular songs. These tabs range in difficulty from modest exercises to extreme examples of classical virtuosity.
https://www.songsterr.com/

<u>Ultimate-Guitar</u>
Ultimate Guitar also provides players with a suite of tabs ranging in both genre and difficulty. This site gives users chord charts with lyrics alongside many different arrangements of popular songs.
https://www.ultimate-guitar.com/

Metronome

<u>The Google Metronome</u>

A simple example of a metronome, this browser-based application provides a quick and easy metronome exclusively in 4/4-time. The tool also features a convenient tempo slider to help you improve your play

https://www.google.com/search?q=metronome

<u>Flutetunes Metronome</u>

While originally built to help flutists practice and analyze their play, this metronome is excellent for any musicians and provides more advanced features than the google example presented above. This metronome also includes a tempo slider, but provides its users with the ability to change time signatures within the click track. Such a feature is invaluable when practicing songs in different time signatures like 3/4, 5/4, or even 12/8.

Glossary of Terms:

Acoustic Guitar Strings:
Strings typically made from combinations of bronze-wound and plain steel that vary in thickness from light- to heavy-string gauge. In most acoustic guitar string sets, the E, A, D, and G strings are wound with bronze while the B and high-E strings are left unwound. A small metal cylinder is secured to the end of each string to help attach the strings to the acoustic guitar.

Acoustic Guitar:
A wooden guitar with a sound hole positioned near the center of its hollow body.

Acoustic Guitar Body:
The largest portion of the acoustic guitar, the acoustic guitar body is made from varying species of wood and absorbs, amplifies, and outputs sound produced by the guitar strings.

Back:
The face opposite the stringed face of the guitar.

Barre Chord:
A guitar chord played with one finger, often the index finger, pressing down multiple strings across a single fret on the fingerboard.

Beat:
A musical division of a measure. The pulse of a song a listener or musician counts rhythm to.

Bridge:
A wooden or metal securing point for strings. The bridge maintains string tension in both acoustic and electric guitars as well as transfers string vibration to the guitar top in acoustic guitars.

Bridge Pins:
Bridge pins, commonly made from wood, plastic, or even bone, secure guitar strings to the acoustic guitar body.

Chord:
A combination of three or more notes played at the same time.

Chord Box (or Diagram):
A diagram that visually explains where a chord is played on the fingerboard, which strings are fretted or unfretted, and which fingers are used to play the chord.

Cleaning Cloth:
A soft, non-abrasive cloth used to clean the guitar without scratching the guitar's finish.

Clip-On Tuner:
A guitar tuner that clips onto the headstock of the guitar. Clip-on tuners measure string vibration frequency and display the frequency, in note value, (ex. A, Db, etc.), on a small digital screen.

Downstrokes:
A picking or strumming motion that starts above the guitar string or strings and picks or strums downward away from your face.

Electric Guitar Body:
The largest portion of the electric guitar, the body provides a support system for pickups, internal wiring, bridge placement, and string connection.

Electric Guitar Strings:
Steel wire cores wound with steel, nickel, or alloys of the two. Electric guitar strings are measured in thickness gauge and range from extra-light to heavy string gauges. Each electric guitar string is fitted with a small, hollow, metal cylinder called the ball-end of the string.

Electric Guitars:
A hollow, semi-hollow, or solid-body wooden guitar with pickups placed between the bridge and the neck.

Fingerboard:
A long, thin wooden slab commonly segmented with metal frets, the fingerboard is where a guitarist frets notes on the guitar.

Frets:
Thin strips of metal that separate the fingerboard into playable segments. The position between the metal frets on the fingerboard.

Fretting Hand:
The hand used to fret notes, chords, and scales on the guitar fingerboard.

Full-Step (or Whole-Step) Bends:
An increase in string tension that raises a note on a given fret and string by one whole step.

Guitar Picks:
Shaped pieces of plastic, wood, metal, glass, and other materials. Guitar picks are used to strum and pluck guitar strings.

Guitar Straps:
Guitar straps secure to strap buttons on opposing sides of the guitar and allow a guitarist to stand while playing.

Guitar Tablature:
Guitar tablature or "TAB", is a method of writing and reading music played on the guitar. Tabs are written with numbers placed individually or in groups across horizontal guitar string lines. These horizontal lines follow the order of the guitar strings, starting with the lowest-pitched strings on the bottom of the guitar tablature and progress to the highest-pitched strings on the top. Modern tabs also include measure lines and bar lines.

Half Step:
A single semitone difference in note value between two notes. On the guitar, a half step increase or decrease would be one fret higher or lower than a starting position.

Half-Step Bends:
An increase in string tension that raises a note on a given fret and string by one half step.

Hammer-Ons:
A guitar technique where a guitarist plucks a fretted string once and uses another finger to rapidly press the same string down on a higher-pitched fret.

Headstock:
A widened wooden section on the end of the guitar neck where tuning pegs are attached to the guitar.

Hollow-Body Guitar:
An electric guitar with a completely hollow body. Hollow-body guitars do not have tone blocks like semi-hollow body guitars.

Instrument Cable:
A cable that transmits signals produced by a guitar to an amplifier, tuner, or a recording device.

Line-In Tuner:
A guitar tuner that uses an instrument cable to determine the pitch of each guitar string. The line-in tuner uses a digital interface to express the current pitch of the guitar strings as they are played.

Measures:
Measures separate music into sections of time based on the time signature of a given musical piece. In 4/4-time a measure is equal to four quarter notes, or note divisions of equal value. Each measure is separated from one another with solid black bar lines.

Metronome:
A practice tool that keeps track of time, musicians set the tempo and time signature on the metronome to suit the musical piece or exercise they are practicing.

Microphone-Based Tuner:
A guitar tuner that uses a microphone to sense and display string vibration frequencies.

Neck:
A long wooden extension of the guitar, the neck of the guitar is half-rounded and half-flat with the headstock positioned on the distal end of the neck. The fingerboard is attached to the flattened side of the neck.

Note:
A written symbol representing a musical pitch. A single sound played on an instrument.

Note - Eighth:
A note equal in time to one-half of a quarter note or two sixteenth notes.

Note - Half:
A note equal in time to one-half of a whole note or two quarter notes.

Note - Quarter:
A note equal in time to one-half of a half note or two eighth notes.

Note - Whole:
A note equal to four quarter notes or two half notes.

Nut:
A piece of notched, hard material placed between the end of the fingerboard and the beginning of the headstock. The nut, in conjunction with the bridge, helps maintain even string spacing along the guitar's neck.

Octave:
Two notes separated by 12 half steps (semitones). (e.g: low-E-String open, 12th fret of the low E-string)

Pentatonic - Minor:
A five-note musical scale built using the following pattern: (W+H), W, W, (W+H), W.

Power Chord:
An interval, often used in rock, metal, and pop genres, consisting of a root note and a perfect fifth interval played simultaneously.

Pull-Offs:
A guitar technique where a guitarist frets a string, plucks the string, removes the finger from the fret, and allows an open or other fretted note to sound without picking again.

Scale:
A series of three or more notes in ascending or descending order.

Scale Diagram:
A grid system with vertical fret lines and horizontal string lines, finger positions, and fingerboard positions. In most scale diagrams, horizontal lines will be oriented with the bottom line of the image denoting the low-E string and the top line representing the high-E string.

Scale Degree:
A note's position within a given scale. For example, in C major (CDEFGABC) F would be the fourth (IV) or subdominant scale degree.

Semi-Hollow Body:
A nearly hollow electric guitar body with a tone-block placed on-center within the guitar's body. The semi-hollow electric guitar body may or may not have F-shaped sound holes carved into the top of the guitar.

Seventh Chords:
A major or minor triad with an added seventh interval.

Slide:
A guitar technique where one note is fretted, plucked, and slid up or down to another note on the fingerboard.

Solid-Body:
An electric guitar body made from solid wood.

Sound Hole:
An opening in a guitar that allows the air resonating within the guitar's sound chamber to transfer to the air outside of the guitar.

Standard Tuning:
A generally acknowledged series of pitches to which guitarists tune their guitars. The tuning: Low-E, A, D, G, B, High-E.

String Gauge:

The thickness of a string, measured in 1/1000th of an inch. (E.g., .009, a very thin or light string gauge, is equal to 9/1000th of an inch.)

Strumming Hand:

The hand used to strum or pluck the strings on a guitar.

Tempo:

The speed at which a song or exercise is played. Tempo is measured in beats per minute or "BPM", for short.

Time Signature:

The numerical representation provided at the beginning, or within, a piece of music that communicates how many beats each measure contains in the top number of the fraction, and which note value a beat is equal to in the bottom number of the "fraction".

Tuning Machines:

A mechanical device used to secure strings to the guitar and adjust string tension.

Upstrokes:

A picking or strumming motion that starts below the guitar string or strings and picks or strums upward toward your face.

Vibrato:

A guitar technique performed using alternating upward and downward bending motions on a given note or series of notes.

Whole Step:

An interval consisting of two semitones or half steps. On the guitar, a whole step is two frets above or below a starting position. (E.g., Low-E string: 5th fret to 7th fret.)

Chord Index

Use this chord index to find the chords detailed within this guide in one location.

Open Chords

Major Shapes

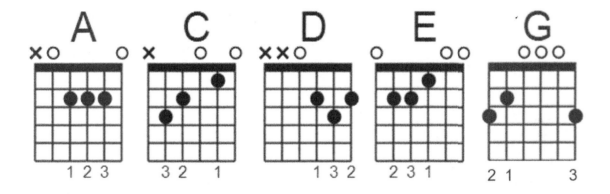

Minor Shapes

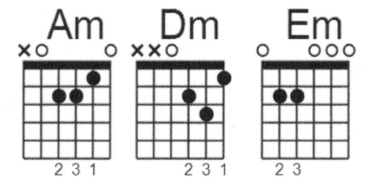

Dominant Seventh Chords in Open Position

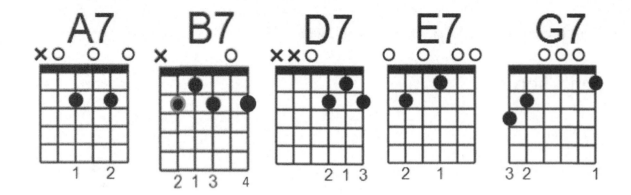

Minor Seventh Chords in Open Position

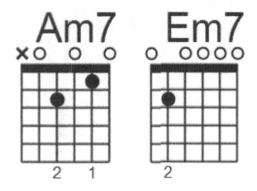

Barre Chord Shapes

Sixth String Major Barre Chords

Sixth String Minor Barre Chords

Fifth String Major Barre Chords

Fifth String Minor Barre Chords